The History of Business and Industry in Jackson, Michigan

by the Ella Sharp Museum

G. Bradley Publishing, Inc.
St. Louis, Missouri

The History of Business and Industry in Jackson, Michigan

by the Ella Sharp Museum

A limited Edition of 2000
in which this is number
1993

Publication Staff
Author: Tom Bohn
Advisors: Gregg Larson and Lynnea Loftis
Cover Artist: Gary Butler
Book Design: Diane Kramer
Publisher: G. Bradley Publishing, Inc.
Sponsors: City Bank & Trust Company and the Ella Sharp Museum

ISBN 0-943-963-34-6
Printed in the United States of America

Table of Contents

Introduction

Through the presentation of images, the chapters that follow attempt to recreate some of Jackson's growth for today's reader. It should be noted that developments within these diverse industries were often inter-related, but due to a "History of Business and Industry's" pictorial focus, the city's various commercial developments have been arranged according to broad themes, such as 'Railroads' or 'Mills and Milling.' A visual record of the growth of Jackson's railroads, the establishment of Michigan's first state prison, the vision of local leaders and entrepreneurs, the discovery of the coal in Jackson County — all of these things and more can be found in the pages that follow.

James Thomas, one of Jackson's earliest historians, looked back on his city's history in 1867 and wrote that "forests which but yesterday were growing to decay, are now employing myriads of men in transforming them into the utilities of civilization; the yell of marauding savages is still fresh on our ears while its echoes are being caught up and re-flung to the winds by the shriek of the locomotive as the thunder of its approach heralds the advent of enlightened industry." Though we ought to dismiss Thomas' evaluation of Jackson's Native American inhabitants as 'marauding savages,' his description of the difference between Jackson's pioneer days and the second half of the nineteenth century should tell us much about our own point of view.

We see Jackson from the vantage point of the late twentieth century. Jackson, like communities throughout the United States, now faces many fresh changes and challenges. The appearance of more powerful computers in the workplace, increased technological sophistication, worldwide competition and the growing importance of environmental technologies will, more than likely, bring many unforeseen innovations to the community's business and industry. To better prepare ourselves for those years to come, let's take a look back, once again, to the years that have already passed us by. Hopefully, such a look back will help us to answer the questions, why here? Why Jackson?

Foreword

History is an ongoing process. Communities grow and change, people adapt, and life goes on. Usually we have little awareness of the significance of the change that goes on around us. That is why it is important that institutions which are involved in interpreting local history, like the Ella Sharp Museum, continue to collect, preserve and exhibit the objects, photographs and documents that record that history. For by looking back, we can gain some perspective — some understanding. Jackson is a community with a rich business history. As we read about this history, and the ability of our city and its people to grasp new ideas and technology, and to take advantage of opportunities, and to react positively to growth and change; we should all feel both a great sense of pride in our past accomplishments and a commitment to the future.

Lynnea Loftis
Director of Collections
Ella Sharp Museum

Panoramic View of the City

# of Jackson, Michigan 1881

Jackson: The Early Years

In looking toward the roots of Jackson's thriving business and industrial community, the question inevitably appears: why here? why Jackson? The question should appeal to us — nearly one third of our life is spent at work or in working situations and our curiosity naturally turns toward the origins of our working experiences. For Jacksonians, those origins were in the early days of Michigan's settlement when, in the late 1820s, settlers from New York and other eastern seaboard states made the long journey overland into the undeveloped Michigan Territory, known then as 'The West.'

The foundation and development of villages and towns in the early American West typically centered around a few vital resources. Fertile land, preferably easily cleared of trees, was the foremost consideration in staking out sites for future inhabitants. Pioneers sought running water — water was needed both as a living resource and as a source of power for early manufacturing technologies. Horace Blackman pounded in the stakes for the 'Jacksonburgh' settlement near the banks of the Grand River in the early months of 1830. The somewhat marshy wetlands that filled the area were complemented by what promised to become fruitful farmland and the river appeared able to provide for a saw mill and a flouring mill. Blackman's location was central to the newly organized Jackson County and to Michigan, as well. But most crucial to the success of Blackman's brand new community were the skills and knowledge brought to it by the settlers themselves.

Some of the supplies and tools needed by Jackson's pioneers were brought from the East, but many others needed to be built, improvised or constructed as Jackson's site required. Blacksmiths were needed to repair tools such as plowshares and cutting edges of all sorts, to make nails and to improvise repairs for wagons and carts. Mechanics made the construction of saw mills and flouring mills a possibility and helped in their repair and maintenance during breakdowns. The woodworking skills of carpenters supplied needed items for new farms and households, while cobblers repaired shoes and made new ones for the feet of growing children. The often -ignored clothmaking and repairing skills brought to the West by women were critical to survival and comfort. Clothing and cloth were some of the early settlers' most valued talents. In addition, skills and knowledge of the 'new' lands, such as local crafting resources, facts concerning weather patterns, edible or dangerous plants and fruits and the most easily traversed lands, were in most cases given readily from Jackson's indigenous inhabitants. Such skills were the most valuable possessions Jackson's pioneers carried with them as they traveled west — the Jackson area's natural resources of wood, flowing rivers, fertile farmland and minerals were useless without the accumulated knowledge that allowed such resources to be enjoyed and used to the settlers' benefit.

Jackson's New England progenitors set about the construction of mills almost immediately after founding the village. All early wood and agricultural milling processes were powered by water or wind: — Horace Blackman's location of Jackson on the banks of the Grand River assured a steady local power supply. The slow-moving current of the Grand River in Jackson made it necessary to dam the river to gain any useful power, and this made competition for the most desirable locations fierce. A group of rival entrepreneurs arrived at the settlement of 'Jacksonburgh' in 1830, hoping to get the jump on Horace Blackman (who had returned to his home in New York to get his family and possessions). Isaiah Bennett and William R. Thompson led a group of mechanics, millwrights and carpenters from Ann Arbor to Blackman's site in Jackson County and they proceeded to build a saw mill, thus planting the seeds for Jackson's industrial future.

Jackson's first flouring mills, William and Jerry Ford's Aetna Mills, were opened seven years later, in 1837. "The matter was placed in charge of William Ford," wrote local historian Charles DeLand. "About fifty men were employed in all the summer (of 1836) and by October first the race was completed and the mills ready to raise ... In July, 1837, the mill was put into operation — the first flouring mill in the city." The opening of the Aetna Mills, coupled with the onrush of settlers brought into Jackson in 1841 with the appearance of the Michigan Central Railroad, brought about Jackson's first great period of economic growth. Many small businesses catered to the needs of settlers moving into Jackson from the East and small local industries produced farm tools, wagons, carts, shoes and other equipment in the city's early 'manufactories.'

In subsequent years, new mills were built, railroad connections were made, numerous businesses had their beginnings in Jackson, and the settlement eventually grew into a thriving industrial center.

Horace Blackman was the first to purchase land and settle his family in Jackson.

Original 1831 plat of Jacksonburg showing settlement along the Grand River.

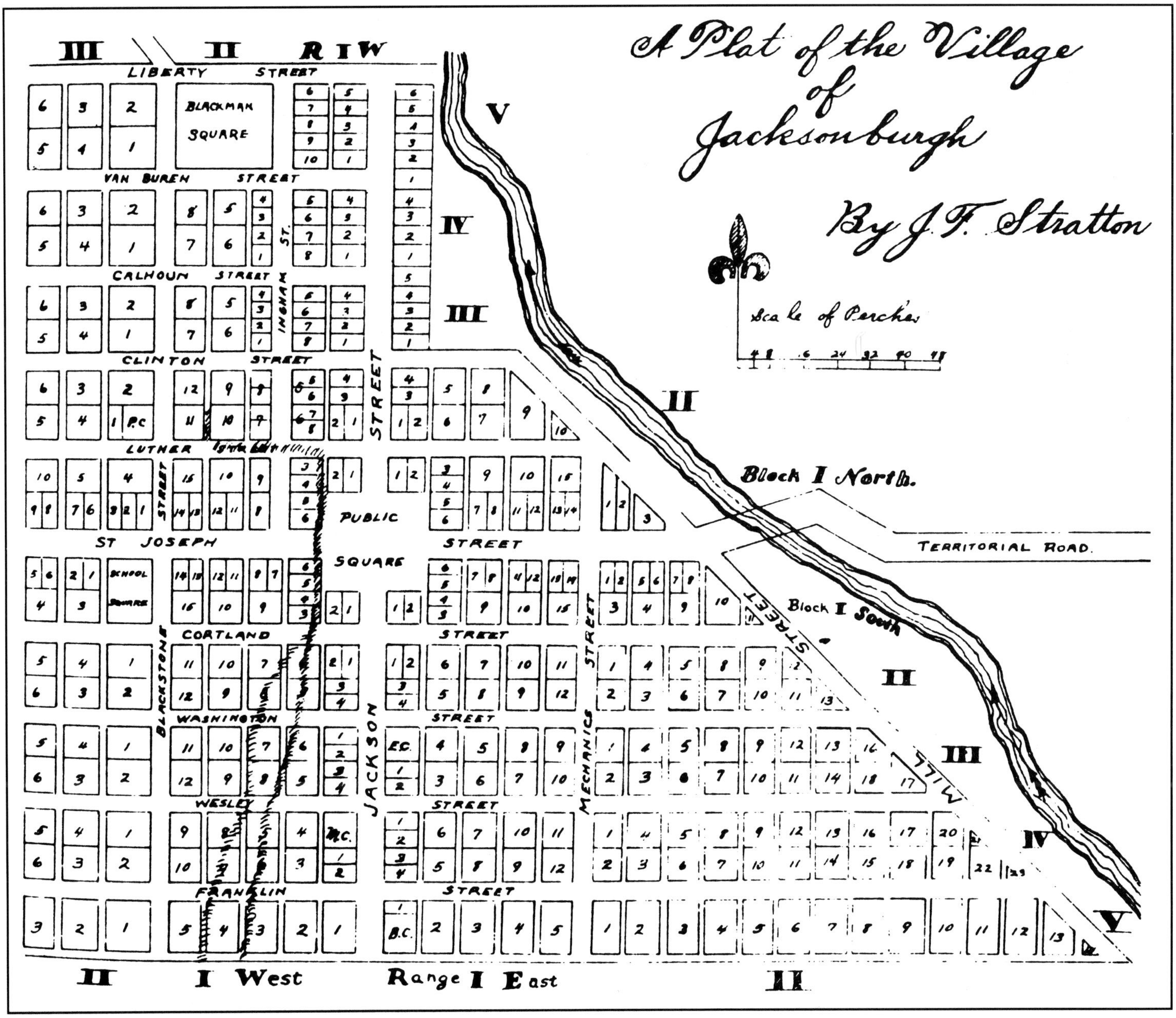

Mills & Milling

During the early years of Michigan's settlement, a community's construction of a flouring mill was an important step toward the way of life the pioneers had known on the eastern seaboard. Building a mill formed a rite of passage: it marked a western community's transition from frontier settlement to pioneering civilization. Without a mill's enormous grindstones, Michigan settlers' wheat, rye, oat and barley crops were edible, but hardly satisfying. The struggling, young 'Jacksonburgh' settlement survived for eight years before the construction of its first flouring mill. It wasn't until 1837, during the peak years of Michigan's settlement, that William and Jerry Ford constructed their Aetna Flouring Mills.

The Ford Mill was the first structure built on the east side of the Grand River and had a capacity of 100 barrels of ground flour per day. The new flouring mill eliminated the need for early Jacksonians to make a costly, three-day trip to Dexter to grind their crops. What was more, the new mill attracted large numbers of settlers to the Jackson area, helping the young community to grow.

The population of Jackson multiplied by leaps and bounds after the arrival of the Michigan Central Railroad in 1841. For the next four years, Jackson was the expanding railroad line's westernmost terminal.

In 1847, John R. Kennedy opened the Kennedy Mills. Unlike the earlier Aetna Mills, the Kennedy Mills were steam-powered. The steam engine used by the Kennedy Mills was manufactured at the Michigan State Prison, and was one of the very first to be put to use in Jackson County. The new mills boosted the village's flour-making capacity and Jackson became very attractive to settlers: ample grain-milling facilities were an important factor in the picking of locations for farms and businesses. An 1847 *Jackson Citizen* article proclaimed that the new mills would make "Jackson turn out as many barrels of flour as any station on the great thoroughfare from Detroit to Chicago during the present fall."

Jackson's milling industry expanded with the growth of the city's industrial resources. William Bennett and Charles Knickerbocker's Jackson City Mills—Jackson's largest—began operations in 1872. The continuing development of rail lines in Michigan and the opening of four new branch lines into the city made Jackson an excellent flour milling location. Wheat and other grain crops could be shipped into the city from the fertile farmlands surrounding Jackson and finished flour could be shipped to outlying markets. This, combined with the opening of numerous coal mines in and around the city helped boost the expansion of Jackson's milling industry.

The city's flour-makers had expanded from the smaller, 100-barrel capacity, waterpowered mills of the 1830s, to huge mills of factory dimensions. The Jackson City Mill's grain elevators held 42,000 bushels of grain and the mill was capable of producing 300 finished barrels of flour daily. Another large grain processor, the Eldred Flouring Mill, was completed in 1888. It was the last large flour-making factory to be built in Jackson and was completely equipped by local machine-making companies.

The enormous success of the milling industy supported several new, local businesses and industries. A group of flouring equipment manufacturers and machinists expanded and flourished as Jackson's flouring mills grew to greater grain capacities. These machine manufacturers designed and developed ways to mechanize the various stages in the milling process, from grinding to sifting. Many small distributors and bakeries also benefitted from the mills' huge success. One bakery, the U.S. Baking Company, grew from a small, local bakery to a four-story bread factory that made everything from the 'Jaxon' cracker to candy, confections and a variety of breads.

Jackson's local millers and flour makers brought their product to the public through small flour and feed stores such as the one pictured here, ca. 1910. G.W. Thorpe's feed and flour 'dealership' was located on N. Jackson Street.

In Jackson's early days, most families ate bread and baked goods made in their own homes. This began to change with the growth of Jackson's mills. The new mills boosted the villages flour-making capacity and Jackson became very attractive to settlers. Ample grain milling facilities were an important factor in picking locations for farms and businesses. In 1847 John R. Kennedy opened the Kennedy Mills.

After 1830, many manufacturers in the United States began turning toward coal-fired steam engines and almost all water-powered mills were eventually converted to steam power. Wooden gears and paddle wheels, like the ones shown in this photograph, were removed and replaced by steam engines.

The Eldred Milling Company finished constructing its milling factory in 1888. This cutaway engraving of the mills appeared in the 1889 *Citizen Industrial Edition*. The mills, owned and operated by Rufus Emerson and S.S. Heywood, were completely equipped by Jackson flouring machinery makers and were capable of finishing 650 barrels of flour per day.

A view of the interior of the Eldred Mills. These 'bolting' machines, built in Jackson by the George T. Smith Middlings Purifier Company, sifted and separated different grades of flour. Roughly ground grain was delivered to the machines through chutes. Revolving, 'bolting' screens then delivered the different sized particles of the flour to various receptacles.

An exterior view of the Eldred Mills around the turn of the century. Besides 'Puritan,' 'Rosebud' and 'Pillsbury's Best' brands of flour, the mills also produced 'Charm' and 'Jackson's Best.'

The Eldred Mills' millwrights and other employees, ca. 1910.

The George T. Smith Middlings Purifier Company

In 1879, Jacksonian George T. Smith perfected a new method for purifying and separating roughly ground flour. Smith's new flouring system was demonstrated in various American cities and later in Britain and Continental Europe as well. The *Jackson Citizen* reported that "Mr. Smith visited the principal countries of Europe introducing his novel inventions and demonstrating to the conservative old world millers the vast superiority of the new American system over their old and decidedly primitive methods of converting grain into flour..." As a local demonstration of the middlings purifier's efficiency, Smith's machinery was used to equip Jackson's massive Eldred Mills.

Smith's machine was built in Jackson and the company thrived, employing over 200 workers in 1888. Management began to look into the possibility of expansion after 1887 and Smith began to spread the news about town: the purifier factory was looking to re-locate. The reaction on the part of the Jackson City Council was swift. "The citizens of the Central City," wrote a *Jackson Citizen* reporter, "fully awake to the importance of the proposed enlargement, placed the matter before the council, resulting in a decision to determine, by popular vote, whether or not the city should purchase the old plant thereby enabling the Purifier Company to rebuild on a scale in keeping with the demands of increased prosperity."

The city financed Smith's expansion and an enormous facility was planned and built. The factory covered more than seventeen acres and included a foundry, dry kilns, several large steam engines and many sub-divided rooms to accommodate production of Smith's contraption. Smith's plant was designed for the employment of 1,000 workers, but his dreams of success were soon dissipated by competition from smaller, local companies. Many new firms began producing less expensive flour-making machinery and the increased competition was too much for the Smith Middlings Purifier Works. Smith went bankrupt, forcing him to sell out, and the city lost its re-financing gamble. The venture wasn't a total loss, however: Smith's enormous factory was to house many later Jackson companies, including the Buick and Briscoe car companies, and the Kelsey-Hayes Company.

George T. Smith organized this small band in 1888. The George T. Smith band traveled the local area, playing for Jacksonians' amusement and advertising the machinery and equipment produced at the emormous 'Purifier Works.'

The original George T. Smith factory as it appeared ca. 1935, long after Smith had vacated the premises.

An engraving of one of the Knickerbocker Company's flour-milling machines. This 'Rotary Sieve' mechanically separated different grades of flour, from fine to rough.

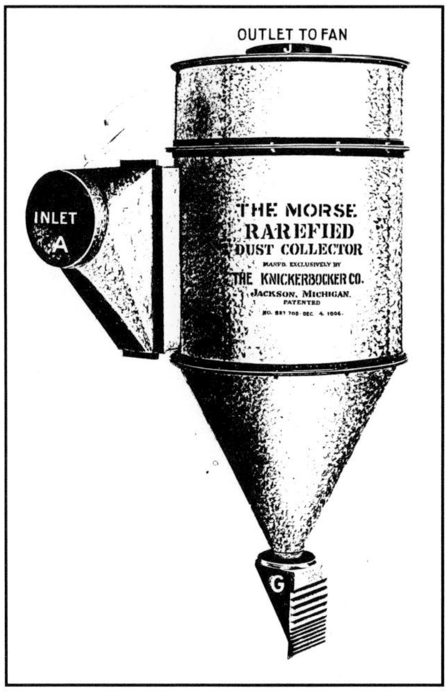

Other Jackson companies produced flour-milling equipment as well. The Charles Knickerbocker Company manufactured both flour purifiers and industrial air cleaners, such as this Morse Rarefied Dust Collector. Knickerbocker continued to grow and, like many other early Jackson manufacturers, eventually began to change its focus from making grain-processing equipment to making other small, metal machinery.

An exterior view of the Harmon Manufacturing Company, ca. 1895. Harmon Manufacturing was established in 1893 by prominent local businessmen S.B. and H.C. Collins. The machine makers produced the Morse Purifier and the Wilson Tubular Dust Collector.

John Hutchinson, founder of the Hutchinson Flouring Machinery Company.

Another of Jackson's large flouring equipment manufacturers, the John Hutchinson Company, was formed in 1882. Hutchinson produced the 'Original Rickerson Six Inch Rolling Mill.' The presence of such agricultural equipment makers in Jackson made the city a base for machine tools and small metal parts manufacturing after the turn of the century. Hutchinson's factory building was later purchased by the Frost Gear and Forge Company.

In Jackson's early days, most families ate bread and baked goods made in their own homes. This began to change with the growth of Jackson's mills.

Jackson's United States Baking Company was formed in 1884 as a small, local bakery. Later, the bakery began viewing its bread, crackers and cookies as manufactured articles. Using enormous quantities of flour — made available by Jackson's high-output flouring industry — the bakery expanded and began mass producing baked goods, shipping them by rail as far away as Indiana and Illinois. This photograph, ca. 1895, shows the exterior of the U.S. Baking Co.'s three-story 'cracker factory.'

M.F. Cottrell,
founder of the Jackson Bakery

Isbell

Among the many businesses in Jackson that centered around agriculture was S.M. Isbell & Company. The business was founded in 1878 by S.M. Isbell on West Pearl Street. The main focus of Isbell's business gradually narrowed from a wide variety of seed stocks to just beans, apples and wool. In 1887, Isbell opened a 'branch' business in Stockbridge and by the late 1890s, had grown to be the state's largest distributor of bean seed stock.

Workers pose near a moving belt, ca. 1895. Beans were processed by an enormous machine that cleaned, graded and sized 200 bushels of beans every hour. They were then run along a moving belt in front of 'pickers,' who then removed any excess dirt or imperfect beans. Isbell was, at one time, the largest bean distributor in the state.

The warehouse and elevator of S.M. Isbell and Company as it appeared in 1912.

The Isbell Seed Company's building on North Mechanic, ca. 1930.

Aspinwall

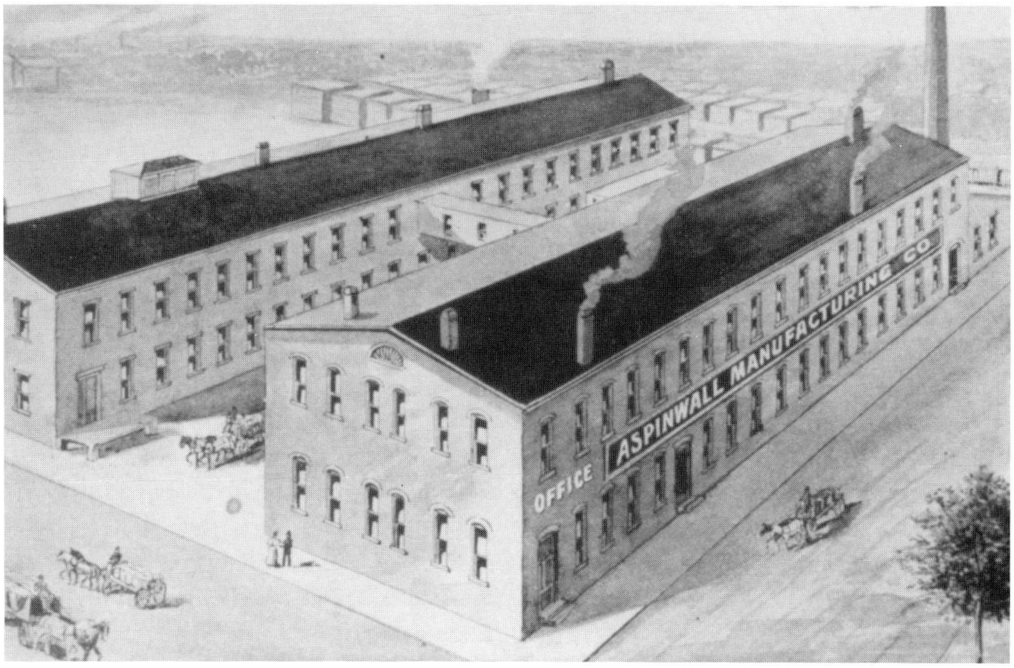

An early engraving, ca. 1884, depicting the factory of the Aspinwall Manufacturing Company, located at the corner of Sabin and Woodbridge.

In addition to flour-making machinery, bakery services and seed stock companies, some of Jackson's earliest industries centered around the machinery used by the farmer in his production of crops. The Aspinwall Manufacturing Company, for example, produced the Aspinwall potato planter: a small wood and metal contraption, operated by foot, which was used by the farmer to plant potato seeds. Such potato-planting gadgets were manufactured throughout the United States, but Aspinwall's product gained a special reputation for itself. The company also produced cutters, fertilizer distributors, seed and potato sorters as well as corn and bean `drills' — machines used to create furrows in the earth and plant seeds at regular intervals and then cover them with dirt. Aspinwall was incorporated in 1884 and moved from Three Rivers, Michigan, to Jackson in 1892 to take advantage of the Central City's superior rail connections. The company was large for its day, employing almost one hundred men and a description of the company, written in 1895, proclaimed that "the Aspinwall planter is a household word as much as the McCormick or Deering harvesters, and every farmer feels that it is a necessary aid in their labors."

The office and distribution house of the Empire Drill Company, ca. 1895. The portrait depicts Charles T. McNolty, Empire's Jackson manager. The Jackson branch of the company served Michigan, Wisconsin, Ohio, Northern Illinois and Indiana.

Coal Mining in Jackson

In the 1860s and 1870s, the move from water-powered to steam-powered machinery, and the growing importance of the railway system to Jackson's industries, created a demand for high volumes of fuel. The earliest businesses in Jackson probably used wood and surface coal deposits to heat their steam boilers. Local coal distributors' advertisements began to appear as early as the 1860s: but coal mining in and around the city became 'big business' in the mid 1880s, when Jackson's flourishing industrial factories created an unprecedented demand for cheap coal. Records dating from 1880 show that an estimated 150,000 tons of coal were taken from the Jackson basin in that year.

Jackson mines were typically sunk with shafts from 15 to 80 feet: the coal was a low-grade bituminous (high in sulfur content) and the seam ranged from one and a half to five feet in thickness —a relatively thin layer. The particular formation of the Jackson coal basin made mining tedious and dangerous.

Miners worked doubled over in the four-foot high shafts, usually while standing in six to twenty-four inches of water. Even more troubling were mine fires and flooding. Temporary, wooden elevator structures were built at the mouth of the mine's shaft and it wasn't unusual for these 'top works' to burn. Flooding was a regular occurence: the wetlands, bogs and marshes of the Jackson area attest to its high water table and water-control was a continual mining problem. One flood, at the Michigan Coal Company's mine in December of 1880, filled the mine with water in a single day: a disaster which took several months to overcome so that mining could be resumed. It was not uncommon for dynamite blasts to loosen the sandstone above the seam, causing shaft collapses.

Because of such hazards, production depended very heavily on the miners' skills. The rigors and hazards of mining work made the job dangerous, but lucrative: Jackson's miners were an exclusive group of highly skilled and well-paid workers. They were also one of the few groups of skilled laborers to unionize during the Knights of Labor organization drives of the 1880s.

The peak of Jackson's coal mining industry came in the late 1880s and early 1890s, though the railroads' and manufacturings' demands for steam power kept the steady mining of Jackson County's bituminous coal a profitable business until almost 1930. By that time, the opening of high-quality anthracite coal mines in the Virginias and the extensive growth of the national rail network had made a higher quality coal inexpensive enough to ship it by rail to the north's industrial cities.

The Sandstone Mine opened in 1857 and operated until shortly before World War I.

Miners often had to work in several inches of water.

Paper & Packaging

The growing manufacturing interests of Jackson created many new local business needs, among them a need for paper and packaging. Several Jackson paper companies appeared, grew and then faded away. One of the first of these, the Emerson Chemical Works, was built in 1870 and produced about three and a half tons of dry wood pulp every day to be used in the making of paper. Jackson's largest paper-making interest was the Jackson Paper Manufacturing Company, founded in 1881. By the late 1890s, the Jackson company was producing eight to ten tons of express wrapping and shipping paper every day. The company sold its products in New York, Boston, Chicago and St. Louis and many prominent Jackson businessmen were part of the company's operations, including the influential Peter B. Loomis. Other paper manufacturers also made Jackson their home for a time, but the city never became a center of paper and packaging production: that role was increasingly taken on by Kalamazoo, which had better geographic and water conditions. Several smaller manufacturers did find a place in Jackson, however, and remained a part of the city's industrial life for many years.

The Louis Blessing Paper and Cigar Box Manufactory made its home in Jackson in 1885. The company produced packaging for many local businesses, but mostly for Jackson's nineteenth century cigarmakers. Though often overlooked, cigar production in Jackson was fairly large in the latter half of the nineteenth century and many brands were produced: the Home Cigar, My Choice, Stein's Own, Romeo and the Central City were just a few. Jackson's cigarmakers were even issued a coveted cigarmaker's union charter. Louis Blessing's paper box factory was the principal packager for such small, boxed items.

The Michigan Bag and Paper Company (originally the Jackson Paper Manufacturing Company) was founded in 1881. The company produced packaging for local companies as well as making paper bags for flour, sugar and other ground products. A specialty of the company was the 'Eveready' line of 'self-opening sugar bags,' sold to a New York sugar distributor.

A view of the entrance to the Michigan State Prison, ca. 1895. The prison's entrance hall was an architectural marvel, attracting thousands of visitors every year. Though the central hall and its attached east wing are no longer standing, the west wing (left) still remains at the north end of Mechanic Street. Note the industrial smokestack rising above the prison's walls.

Michigan's State Prison

The location of Michigan's first state prison in Jackson in 1838 gave the community an advantage over its neighboring villages. Leaders from Marshall, Napoleon, Jackson, Lansing and other central Michigan communities had campaigned vigorously for their village to be the prison's location. $40,000 — a large sum of money in 1838 — had been appropriated as funds for building the prison and local leaders realized the immediate prosperity it would bring to their village. When several Jackson landowners donated almost sixty acres of land to the state, the Michigan legislature decided in favor of Jackson as the prison's location, creating construction, maintenance, food service and administrative jobs. Even more important, however, the Auburn-based system of discipline chosen for the State Prison required that its convicts be put to work on contract for private businesses. The decision to use an Auburn-based system made a large number of inexpensive laborers available in Jackson during a time when such workers were quite scarce.

Two penal systems were in use at the time of the State Prison's planning and construction. In 1837, a team of Michigan legislators, including new Prison Commissioner Benjamin Porter, had been assigned the job of traveling to New York and to Pennsylvania to see the penitentiaries there and to report back to the Michigan state legislature on which architectural style and which disciplinary system seemed most appropriate for Michigan. Porter's team reported back in favor of the Auburn prison system.

Both the Auburn prison in New York and the Pennsylvania prison in Philadelphia maintained a strict disciplinary code of individual confinement during evening and night with no inter-personal communication between prisoners allowed. Both prisons required their convicts to work at hard labor. The difference between the two came in their methods of working the convicts. The Pennsylvania system advocated isolated labor in the solitude of the cell to promote reflection and to guard against any possible talking between prisoners; construction of individual work areas was expensive. The Auburn system, by contrast, worked its prisoners in common groups and usually on contract to private businesses who were given state-provided workshops and resources. The money collected from the convict labor contracts was then used to pay for the cost of maintaining the prison.

A typical contract during the Michigan prison's early years, put from thirty to one hundred and twenty convicts at the disposal

Alonzo Ferris, the first warden of the State Prison. The term 'warden' didn't come into usage until around 1880: before that, the prison's director was known as the 'Agent,' because of his role in contracting prisoners to outside manufacturers.

of an outside employer at rates as low as thirty-three cents per prisoner, per day—a rate much cheaper than the cost of free laborers. Some of Jackson's largest nineteenth century industries got their start in the prison's shops. Farm tools, wagons, carriages, furniture, shoes and many other products were made there. Jackson's two largest nineteenth century companies, the Withington-Cooley Company and the Austin, Tomlinson and Webster Company, had their start at the prison's convict labor shops. The specialties of these companies helped to establish Jackson as a center for the manufacture of farm tools, wagons and carriages.

It would be no exaggeration to say that the prison vastly accelerated Jackson's industrial development. The first steam engines used in the village were manufactured at the prison shops of the Pinney-Connable Company in 1847. They were installed in the flouring mills built by John Kennedy in that year. The *Jackson Citizen* wrote glowing reports of the new steam engines and said that "if the new engine works as well as the one in the State Prison we should expect to see quite a steam raised in this village before long." What is more, the early shops within the state prison were employment giants in comparison to those on the outside, which typically employed no more than ten persons. As the population of the prison grew, so too did the size of its contractors' shops. By the end of the nineteenth century, the Austin, Tomlinson and Webster company employed as many as 140 prisoners, in addition to many free laborers.

The large size of the shops proved to be a disciplinary problem for the prison's administration. Convicts were not supposed to talk to one another and the amount of work they performed was supposed to be strictly enforced. This wasn't always the way things worked out, however, due to the practical needs of the contractors. In 1847, an investigation of the prison's shop discipline was made by the prison Board of Control: the results showed that prisoners often went unsupervised, that they talked freely with one another and with guards, and that they sometimes received private bonuses from their employers. For example, foremen from the prison's barrel-making shops reported that the prisoners would often talk and leave the shops in unsupervised groups and the keeper of the prison's wagon shops testified that "the rules of the prison are not enforced as they ought to be — prisoners are allowed to converse on any subject they choose to, of late, in the yard and in the shops." As a result of the investigation, discipline was tightened and the prison's shops were rearranged to facilitate 'keeping an eye on the prisoners.'

The prisoners sometimes reacted to disciplinary crackdowns by destroying the equipment of contractors. In 1852, a fire destroyed several buildings of the Austin, Tomlinson and Webster wagon shops and they had to be completely rebuilt. Investigations showed that the fire

The Jackson Wagon, produced by the Austin, Tomlinson and Webster Company, became one of the State Prison's most famous products. Thousands were produced by the prison contractor during the second half of the nineteenth century and the sturdy wagons became a favorite with pioneers of the Western states.

was intentionally started by a convict in the employment of the wagon contractors. In order to avoid such disasters, private contractors would sometimes pay their workers with small cash bonuses. Almost fifteen years after the fire of 1852, the prison's Board of Control investigated reports of such activity and found that many of the contractors had been paying cash bonuses to the inmates to get more and better work from them. The board disapproved of the practice, believing that prisoners should not be allowed working time toward their own interests: the small incentives the prisoners had been earning for themselves were ordered discontinued. Not more than a month after the ruling went into effect, the entire set of contractors' shops and buildings burnt to the ground, costing the state and the contractors almost $100,000.

Beyond such problems, however, the prison and its contract system continued to thrive in Jackson. Some troubles arose during the economic hard times of the late 1870s, however, when free laborers in not only Jackson, but in Detroit and Grand Rapids, began to complain that it was unfair to give work to prisoners when no work could be found for freemen. Detroit shoemakers' unions were especially unhappy with the prison's shoe-making contractors. The public debate over the contract labor system appeared in newspapers all over the state and there was some discussion among state legislators of abolishing the prison's contract system. Improvements in the national and state economy, however, lessened the importance of the issue and contract labor continued at the prison. The controversy flared again after the turn of the century and a mounting public pressure to end the contract system —considered by many to be unfair competition with free labor — culminated in the state legislature's eradication of the contract system in 1909. Several contracts stayed in effect until almost 1918.

Following the abolition of the contract system, prisoners were employed by the state on farms and in manufacturing plants owned and operated by the state. Prisoners made a diverse run of products: binder twine, chairs and other furniture, boxes, stone monuments, brooms, brick and tile, among other things. The construction of the new State Prison of Southern Michigan, begun in 1924, brought with it increased expansion of prison manufacturing and new administrative duties. Though prison labor no longer proved a benefit to Jackson's private industries, the prison remained one of the community's largest employers.

Getting In and Out

The prison was directly connected to Jackson's many railroad services: train cars were backed through these gates in the prison's wall, to be loaded with goods produced at the factories inside.

Deliveries of food and manufacturing supplies that didn't come in by rail were made to the prison through the east gate. This picture, ca. 1910, shows the double iron doors that ensured no prisoners escaped along with the horse-drawn wagons. Note the sign in the lower left hand corner announcing "Prison Officials Only."

Prison Life

Though prisoners were put to hard labor during the day, in the evenings and afternoons, some leisure activities were availaable to them. This band, photographed ca. 1910, played for the prisoners' enjoyment.

The Michigan State Prison's baseball team, The Clippers, ca. 1910.

Prisoners cooked most of their own food. Below, convicts prepare bread in the prison's bakery for the day's consumption.

Cell blocks (above) were added to the Michigan State Prison, throughout its years, as the prison's population expanded. In the prison's very early years, few cells were needed: there were only eighty-six prisoners in 1842. But following the close of the Civil War, the prison's population steadily increased, year after year, and appropriations were consistently made to enlarge the institution's capacity. At one point, in 1857, special facilities were built to house Michigan's life sentence prisoners (the death penalty had been abolished in Michigan in 1846). "In 1861," wrote Warden Harry H. Jackson in 1925 "it was realized that to confine men in these dungeons was barbarous and inhumane, and as a result the legislature granted the Agent the right to remove such prisoners and place them at work. There were twenty such convicts, nine of whom were insane."

Convicts in Michigan's State Prison at Jackson ate their meals en masse, entering the dining hall in shifts for breakfast, lunch and dinner.

A Small Industrial Town

For all intents and purposes, the State Prison contained a small manufacturing town. These views of the prison's interior show several of the streets that criss-crossed the six acres of land enclosed by the prison's walls.

Companies like the Withington-Cooley Company, makers of iron forks, hoes and rakes, were some of the first in Jackson to fully mechanize their production. As early as 1860, the Withington-Cooley shops had been specialized into various departments, including this one, the polishing shop. Here, convict employees gave Withington-Cooley farm tools their final polish with the aid of mechanized emery wheels.

Most of the industrial workshops inside of the prison were powered by a single, large steam engine, though some of the contractors supplied their own power. Here, a prisoner is shown near the coal-fired ovens which were used to heat the enormous engine's boilers.

A photograph of the state prison's furniture manufacturing area, ca. 1910. The Gilbert, Ransom and Knapp Company were the first manufacturers of furniture to utilize Jackson's contract labor system. They had sales rooms at 243 and 258 Michigan Avenue, as well as in downtown Battle Creek and Kalamazoo. The *Jackson City Directory* for 1869 proclaimed that Gilbert, Ransom and Knapp's was "the largest manufacturing firm of its kind in the west...The shops produce every day 60 bedsteads, 500 chairs of different kinds, 30 wash stands, 15 to 20 tables of different styles and 25 center tables." Larger furniture was also made, such as bedroom sets, bureaus and dining tables. Later the Michigan Seating Company used convict labor to produce imitation wicker furniture. Michigan Seating was using convict labor as late as 1916.

Among the many types of industry carried on in the prison's shops was stone-cutting and the production of marble monuments. This interior view shows the stone-cutting and shaping room. Note the railroad tracks which run along the floor — marble slabs were carted into the working area on these tracks.

The various manufacturers located in the state prison were some of the first in Jackson to begin mechanizing their production on a large scale. This interior of the Withington-Cooley shops, in particular, were extremely mechanized. Descriptions from as early as 1869 reported grinding, bending, cutting and shaping machines as well as steam-run trip hammers and polishing machines. Withington-Cooley's production capacities rose sharply with their mechanization and James Thomas, an early Jackson historian, wrote in 1869 that "This season Messrs. Withington, and Cooley Co. has slipped large quantities of their wares to England and are receiving larger and larger orders from over the sea! Can any better proof be furnished of the superiority of their manufactures than this? What honor to Jackson and its mechanics, that they are able to successfully compete with the skilled labor of the oldest and most famous artisans of the world!"

From the very beginning, Michigan state prisoners have worked on farms to produce their own food. After 1909, however, fewer prisoners were at work on manufacturing contracts and additional farmland was purchased by the state. Within several years, more food was being produced on the prison's farms than the convicts could consume. A canning factory was started to use the surplus produce and it soon became a profitable business, selling its products to grocery stores throughout the state.

A view from inside the new prison under construction, ca. 1925.

Over-crowding in the old state prison prompted the state legislature to appropriate funds in 1920 for new construction. There were 1,099 prisoners housed in the old Mechanic Street facility. The prison commission planned a new prison with a holding capacity of 5,300. Construction began in 1924 and twelve cell blocks were constructed with capacities of from 380 to 510 prisoners. The palatial residence in the foreground (below) housed the prison's warden. Note the swimming pond.

The New Prison's Canning Factory

This mechanical sorter separated peas according to size.

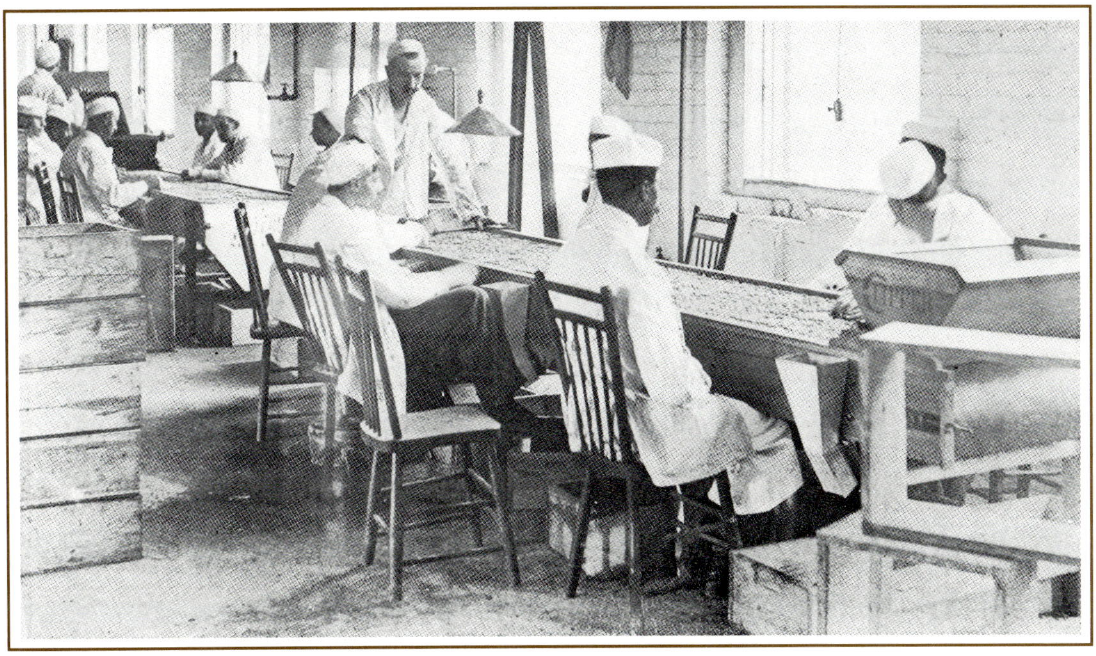

Prisoners, seated before moving belts, picked out imperfect, dirty and rotten vegetables before they were canned.

These enormous boiling vats were used both to blanch vegetables and to sterilize the finished cans.

One of the prison industries most familiar to citizens "on the outside" was making license plates and road signs.

This plant, at Onandaga, was constructed in 1918 to house the Michigan state brick and tile factory. Over one hundred prisoners were employed at the facility, which was located almost twenty miles north of the prison. The brick and tile plant operated successfully until 1924, when a boycott by organized labor, against bricks made by prison labor, made the Onandaga operation unprofitable.

Prisoners tended these twine-winding machines.

Bailed twine was stored in the prison's warehouses.

One of the most successful Michigan state prison industries was the Binder Twine Factory. Convicts produced a rough, woven twine that was sold to farmers throughout the country for bailing hay and other uses. The plant was started in 1907, and over the years produced an average of eight million pounds of twine every year.

Another view of the binder twine mill.

Bucket Grounds

The Michigan Central Railroad ran directly past the prison, picking up freight from the prison's manufacturing complex along the way. The continuing development of railroad connections in Jackson allowed for an expansion of production not only at the prison's shops, but in manufacturing institutions throughout the city.

Jackson Rides the Rails

Railroads had a bit of a troubled start in the state of Michigan. State planners dreamed of three or four great 'through lines' to be projected across Michigan's interior, connecting the shores of the Detroit River to Lake Michigan, providing a link between eastern cities like Buffalo and New York and the growing American West. Continued political troubles plagued the government line and construction of the railroads proceeded at a snail's pace. Only one of the four planned state lines, the Michigan Central Railroad, reached fruition: work was begun in 1833 and the rail line began to slowly creep westward.

It wasn't until 1841 that the steam and roar of a locomotive was heard in Jackson. The Michigan Central Railroad had arrived, and Jackson remained the rail-line's western terminus for several years: a situation that brought a flood of settlers, prospectors, pioneers and entrepreneurs to Jackson. A stream of population poured from densely populated eastern cities into the newly settled Michigan West. The Michigan Central railway brought a prosperous time to Jackson: the railroad brought needed services, repairwork, metal-shaping and foundry capabilities, freight-shipping and an increasing tourist trade. All of these worked to bring commercial success to many of the city's established businesses and growing industries.

By 1846, state administrative and financial troubles forced the Michigan government to sell its interests in the Michigan Central. New York businessman James F. Joy and several partners continued to privately develop the railway and in 1849 it reached booming Chicago. The resulting increase in freight and trade between Detroit and Chicago along the line made Jackson a desirable site indeed: perceptive, local entrepreneurs began to see the city's future as a rail center. Jackson's central position in the state made it an ideal shipping location and several influential Jackson citizens began to work toward making their city Michigan's foremost railroad town.

Until 1856, the Michigan Central held a monopoly over railroad transportation services in Jackson. In that year, however, a second line — the Michigan Southern — completed a branch line into the city, making Jackson the first settlement in Michigan to be serviced by two competing lines. Two Jacksonians, Dr. Moses A. McNaughton and Amos Root, were instrumental in the completion of the Michigan Southern's branch line. A great celebration was held, sponsored by McNaughton and Root, to commemorate the completion of the new rail service branch. Jackson's prominent citizens, Michigan's governor, Austin Blair, and other notables made a round trip to Toledo and back to Jackson for a feast in D.B. Hibbard's Bronson Hall.

"Over five hundred persons were seated at the table, and the merits of the supper was [sic] heartily and satisfactorily discussed," reported the *1867 Jackson City Guide and Directory*. Toasts were proclaimed all around and the event marked the beginning of the 'railroad fever' in Jackson.

TIME FOR RUNNING TRAINS.

TRAINS WESTWARD. Freight.		Kalamazoo Passenger.		Through Passenger			TRAINS EASTWARD. Through Passenger		Kalamazoo Passenger.		Freight.	
7.	A. M.-Leave.	4.15	P. M.-Leave.	7.30	A.M.-Leave.	Detroit	7.30	P. M.-Arrive.	11.15	A. M.-Arrive.	3.45	P. M.-Arrive
7.52	Follow Pass.	4.40		7.52	Pass Freight	Dearborn	7.7		10.52		3.	
8.43		5.		8.10		Wayne	6.50		10.35		2.25	
10.7	Meet Pass	5.35		8.40		Ypsilanti	6.25		10.7	Meet Freight	1.25	
10.55		6.00	Meet Pass	9.		Ann Arbor	6.	Meet Pass	9.45		12.40	P. M.
11.50	Meet Freight	6.25		9.22	Meet Pass	Dexter	5.37		9.22	Meet Pass	11.50	Meet Freight
12.30	P. M.	6.43		9.40		Chelsea	5 22		9.2		11.10	
1.22		7.7		10.5	Meet Freight	Grass Lake	4.55		8.35		10 5	Meet Pass
2.10		7 35		10.30		Jackson	4.30		8.10		8.55	
3.		8.		*10.53		Parma	4.5		7.42	Pass Freight	7.42	Follow Pass
3.45	Meet Pass	8.23		11.17		Albion	3.45	Meet Freight	7.20		6.40	
4.45 6.50	P. M.-Arrive AM MtP's.Lv.	9.5	SUPPER	12.5	P. M.-DINE.	Marshall	3.20	DINE.	6.50	BR'KFST MtFt	5.30 5.	A.M.-Leave P.M.-Arrive
8.50		9.35		12.35		Battle Creek	2.25		6.		3.45	
9.20		10.10		1.5		Galesburg	1.55		5.25		2.25	
10.10		10.30	P.M.-Arrive	1.32	Mt Pass&Fr'gt	Kalamazoo	1.32	MtPs.&PassFt	5.	A. M.-Leave.	1.32	P.M.Mt&F'lPs
11.55	Meet Freight			2.7		Paw Paw	1.2				11.55	Meet Freight.
12.45	P.M.-Meet Pas.			*2.25		Decatur	12.45	Meet Freight			11.10	
1.40				2.48		Dowagiac	12.17	P. M.			10.10	
2.40				3.41		Niles	11.52				9.	
3.10				3.23		Buchanan	11.37					
3.38	Follow Pass			3.38	Pass Freight	Terre Coupee	11.25				8.	
5.				4.11		New Buffalo	10.50				6.35	
5.50 6.	P. M.-Arrive A. M.-Leave.			4.35		Michigan City	10.30				5.45 6.15	A.M.-Leave P.M.-Arrive
7.10				5.	Meet Freight	Porter	10.				5.	Meet Pass
8.				5.20		Lake	9.38				4.5	
9.15	Meet Pass			5.45		Gibson's	9.15	Meet Freight			3.	
10.				6.5		Junction	8.55				2.10	
11.	A. M.-Arrive.			6.30	P.M.-Arrive	Chicago	8.30	A.M.-Leave			1.	P.M.-Leave.

M. C. R. R. OFFICE, *Detroit, December 3, 1852.*   J. W. BROOKS, *Supt.*

This 1852 train schedule shows the Michigan Central's Jackson itinerary. In the same year, Jackson city officials installed the first public town clock. Before the widespread use of the railroad, every town, village or city was on its own, particular time schedule. It was eventually discovered that a standardized, accurate and precise system of time-keeping was necessary to avoid accidents. Within thirty years Jackson, along with the rest of the nation, adopted standard time — a development that was sparked on by the confusions and collisions that rail lines encountered.

After the Civil War, the United States experienced an unprecedented railroad-building boom. In pre-Civil War Michigan there had been less than 1,000 miles of railroad track, but by 1890, almost 9,000 miles of track had been constructed. Jackson continued to be an important part of Michigan's railroad development and by 1871, another four lines connected the city to the north, south, east and west. Several other connections were made just outside of the city, bringing a grand total of eight available railroads in 1871: Jackson had become Michigan's 'Central City.'

The teeming lines radiating from Jackson's then-thriving downtown manufacturing district carried the city's products throughout Michigan, and eventually brought Jackson-made items to other states, even other countries. The transportation facilities made available by the railroad pushed Jackson's industries to expand. Possibly railroading's biggest boost to

Jackson members of the International Association of Machinists pose for a photograph in 1911. Many of the machinists working in Jackson's railroad shops were I.A.M. members.

Jackson's manufacturers' era came with the Michigan Central's re-location of their locomotive and repair shops from Marshall to Jackson in 1871. The shops eventually brought over one thousand jobs to the community, many of them involving skilled work. Mechanics, engineers, foundry specialists and other knowledgeable skilled workers contributed to the growing economy of Jackson. Their 'know-how' significantly helped the expansion of the city's industries.

McNaughton and Root

During the period between 1865 and 1871, four new rail lines were either built out of Jackson or connected the city to other lines through branch extensions. Several prominent Jackson citizens were key figures in this railroad development, among them Amos Root and Dr. Moses McNaughton. Joining with Peter Loomis — at that time, Jackson's mayor — Root and McNaughton began to put together plans for a rail line between Jackson and Grand Rapids. They only had one problem: they didn't have any money.

Determined to build the line, Root and McNaughton enlisted Loomis' help in gaining 'municipal aid' for the project. Many Jacksonians were, however, less than fond of their 'municipal aid' ideas. Many of the town's businessmen believed their trade would suffer, especially those located on the city's north side: they relied on their customers' lack of transportation into downtown Jackson. Henry Hayden, a Jackson mill owner, was in possession of a seat of the state legislature at the time. When approached by Root and McNaughton, he agreed to introduce a bill to set guidelines and precedents for municipal aid package deals. But Hayden wasn't interested in the bill; in fact, he opposed it.

When Root and McNaughton failed to hear anything about the bill's introduction, they became nervous and began to wonder if the wool wasn't being pulled over their eyes. On the day before the last day of the legislature's 1863 session, McNaughton and Root took a stage to Lansing, arriving at the legislature around 10:00 in the evening only to find no bill introduced and no intention of any bill being passed. Not only was Hayden opposed, but the Lansing representatives were as well, fearing that a line to Grand Rapids would stunt Lansing's business development.

Root and McNaughton immediately sent notice to the Secretary of the Senate that a bill would be introduced by title and they began writing its details. They planned to take advantage of the 'railroad fever' that had struck Michigan and outlined a bill that provided for a line from Jackson to Lansing, instead of Grand Rapids. And so the Jackson, Lansing and Saginaw Railroad Company was enthusiastically formed with

Amos Root

View of the Michigan Central Railroad Shops

Henry Hayden as president! Root and McNaughton were careful to include a clause allowing for the people who were voting the aid to dictate terms and 'one condition was made that the company receiving the aid (the Jackson and Lansing company) should so locate and construct its road as to make it convenient to run the cars of the Grand River Valley Road over it for a distance of ten miles.'

Only three years after the passage of the bill, Jackson and Lansing were connected by rail and a branch was given to the Grand River Valley Road. With legislative sanction, Root and McNaughton began constructing their line and received ten free miles of track, to boot! They began raising capital from interested villages, towns and cities along the route and the line reached Grand Rapids in 1870.

An eight-member Michigan Central Railroad repair gang outside of the M.C.R.R. rail shops.

An interior view of the Michigan Central Railroad shops. Originally located in Marshall, the shops were moved to Jackson in 1871 due to the 'Central City's' superior rail connections and central location. The shops brought thousands of skilled jobs to the Jackson community and helped to establish a long-lasting tradition of engineering and machine design in the city.

The railroads prompted many new types of transportation services in Jackson. These advertisements, ca. 1868, were for stage rides to towns and villages not serviced by the railroads. The Morris Knapp stage line took passengers west to Kalamazoo, and even the Lake Michigan coastline, during the years when the Michigan Central made its last stop in Jackson. Stage lines such as these were important transportation links during the early days of the railroad when line construction was very expensive. Eventually, as costs dropped, many small towns and villages were serviced by their own branch lines and side stops.

Below: The railroads changed the ways people were transported from place to place including within the city limits. This picture, ca. 1886, shows a horse-drawn street car on rails. Cars such as this one were later electrified and they became traction 'trolleys,' named for the sparking trolley device that rolled along the electrical lines. Electric powered 'interurbans' were later installed: they carried passengers by rail from one city to the next. Jackson was connected to Detroit, Kalamazoo and Lansing by such 'interurban' lines.

A Michigan Central locomotive outside of Jackson on its way to Chicago. Trains ran between Detroit and Chicago on a daily basis, stopping in Jackson for passengers and freight.

The Michigan Central Rail Depot, built in 1873, was the largest stop on the line between Detroit and Chicago.

This advertisement for the Smith Bros. and Collins Transfer Company appeared in the 1897 *Polk's City Guide and Directory*. With nine rail connections into Jackson, freight transfer and shipping became one of the city's biggest businesses.

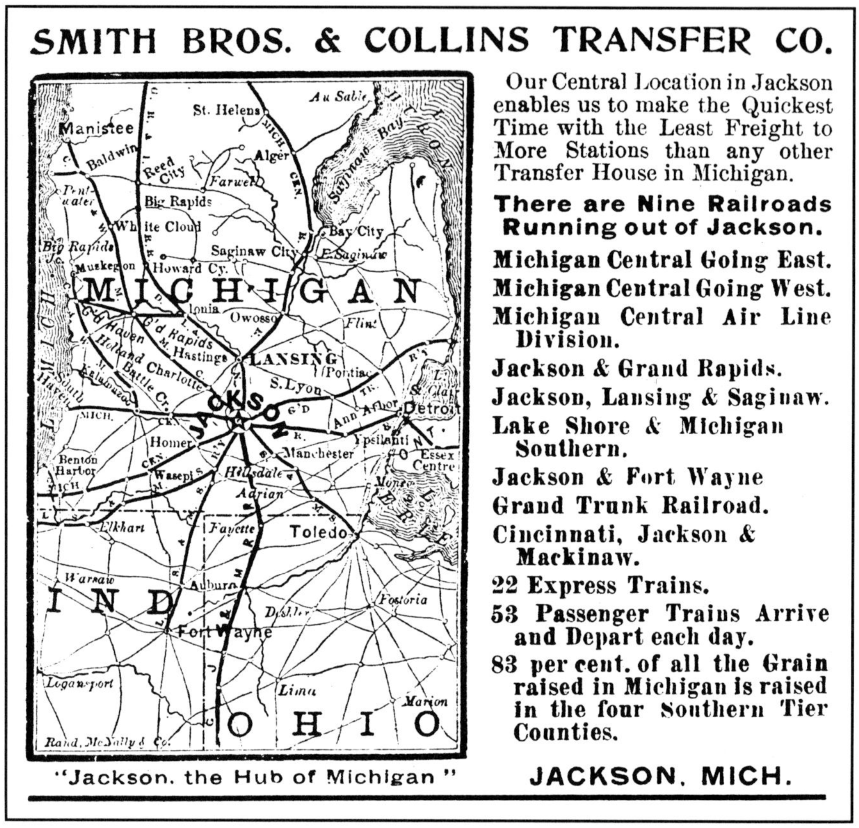

Dwight Smith, one of the Smith-Collins company founders.

This photograph shows the exterior of the Smith Brothers and Collins Transfer Company rail yards and storage docks, as they appeared in 1895. The warehouse had a 50,000 square-foot interior and side tracks running up to two sides of the building. Much of Jackson County's grain crops and other harvests were brought to this building to be shipped to Toledo, Detroit, Chicago and other cities.

This advertisement showing Jackson's railroad connections appeared in the Michigan Central Railroad's *Headlight* magazine in 1895. The magazine was devoted to 'Sights and Scenes Along The Michigan Central Line' and it highlighted Jackson's attractions both for living and business purposes.

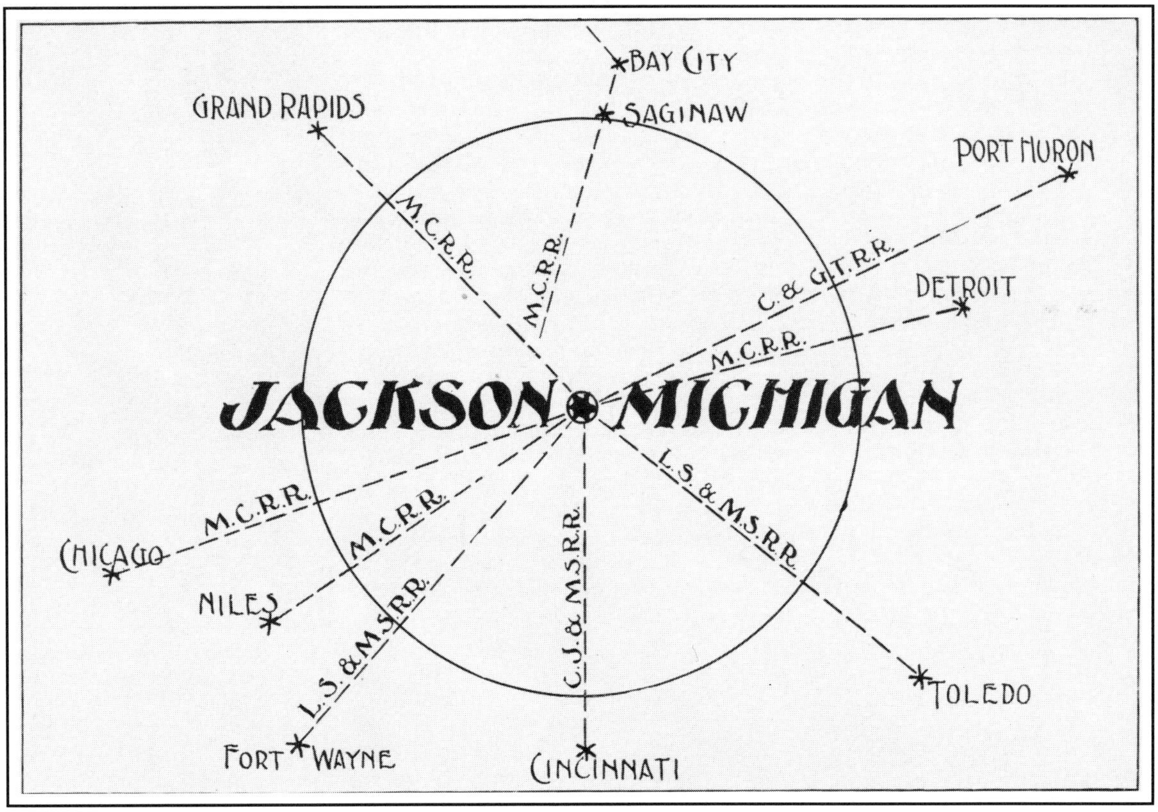

The railroads brought problems as well as prosperity. This photograph, taken in 1893, shows one of Jackson's largest and most sensational train wrecks. A train carrying passengers on their way to the Chicago World's Fair crashed into another train that had stopped in the Michigan Central Railroad's Jackson yards. Thirteen people were killed and the incident became known in Jackson as "The World's Fair Wreck." Wrecks weren't the only problem associated with the railroads: the infamous 'Great Railroad Conspiracy Trial' of 1851 stands out as an example. During the Michigan Central's first few years of service through Jackson, many farmers lost money when their livestock were killed by rushing locomotives and in retaliation, they destroyed railroad property and took pot shots at passing trains. After a fire destroyed a Detroit rail freight depot in 1851, fifty Jackson County citizens were arrested and taken to Detroit where Abel Fitch, a Michigan Center farmer, died of dysentery. The particularly active and outspoken Jackson farmers were blamed for the fire and twelve of the fifty were convicted, though none served complete prison terms. Despite the hostilities that arose from time to time, the relationship between the railroads and the Jackson community was, for the most part, mutually beneficial.

Mechanics, such as these posed in this photograph, were a crucial part of keeping the railroads running smoothly. Steam locomotives were notorious for their maintenance needs and the MCRR repair shops in Jackson were kept busy with constant upkeep, repairs and construction of new steam locomotives.

In 1904, Jackson's shops produced their last steam engines, but continued service and maintenance for Michigan locomotives. Despite this, the city remained an important railroad center: in 1910, almost seventy passenger trains and over one hundred freight trains ran through the city every day. By 1930, most of Jackson's rail service had been acquired by the New York Central Railroad and most of the engines used were purchased from other cities.

The numerous rail lines radiating out of "The Central City" proved to be an enormous boost to Jackson's manufacturing enterprises. Many of Jackson's small shops grew into thriving factories with the introduction of the railroad's shipping services. As the automobile and truck became more popular as shipping vehicles, the importance of the railroad began to decline. The city's rail connections remained important, however, through the 1960s and 1970s, and continue to serve as important transportation lines today.

A group of New York Central Railroad machinists and boiler makers, ca. 1934.

The railroad couldn't run without repairs. The interior of the Michigan Central Railroad shops was always a busy place. Note the huge locomotive being lifted off the ground by strong pulleys.

The New York Central's famous *Twentieth Century Express* steams into Jackson, ca. 1935. As automobiles grew in popularity and availability, use of trains as passenger vehicles dropped dramatically, though they were still widely used by industry for freight transportation.

Carriages, Carts, &

Jackson's first wagonmakers were proprietors of very small and personal businesses. These wood and metal-working artists made carriages and carts by hand, one at a time, for local sale. Their skills were inherited through centuries-old traditions and were employed in modest `manufactories.' National changes were in the air, however, that urged Jackson's makers of horse-drawn vehicles to expand their small shops until they resembled today's factories.

As more and more settlers moved out of the East into Michigan during the 1830s and 1840s, the demand for transportation increased. The pace of westward migration was quickened by the railroad's booming nationwide expansion, and Jackson's buggy and carriage shops changed dramatically. In addition, between 1885 and 1900, eight new companies were founded: the most successful of Jackson's growing carriage and wagonmakers went on to become large organizations that produced thousands of vehicles every year.

In 1895, a Michigan Central Railroad magazine writer described one of Jackson's most important businesses: "In the early days good carriages were largely made by hand..." His introduction tells us of the manufacturing changes that had taken place: the hand-made carriages of the 'early days' had been replaced by the mass-produced, machine-made carriages of 1895. These large-scale makers of wagons, sleighs and buggies established Jackson as a center of transportation manufacturing and contributed to the city's later automobile industry.

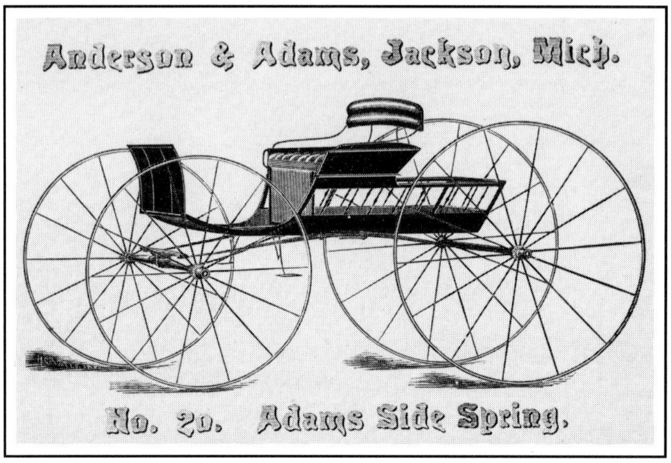

An engraving illustrating an Anderson and Adams Carriage Manufactory specialty. The company was founded in 1871 by John Anderson, a native of New York, and the shop was typical of Jackson's smaller, craft-style carriage makers. Anderson employed from 6 to 18 men, making all sorts of specialty carriages — usually for local sale.

This photograph shows the Thorpe Carriage Company facilities as they appeared in 1895. Thorpe typified Jackson carriage makers during their late nineteenth century heyday. The company employed almost 200 workers, covered 152,000 feet of floor space, produced almost 6,000 horse-drawn vehicles every year and distributed its products throughout the United States.

Wagons

An advertisement for the Hanaw 'Combination Speeder.'

Ferdinand Hanaw

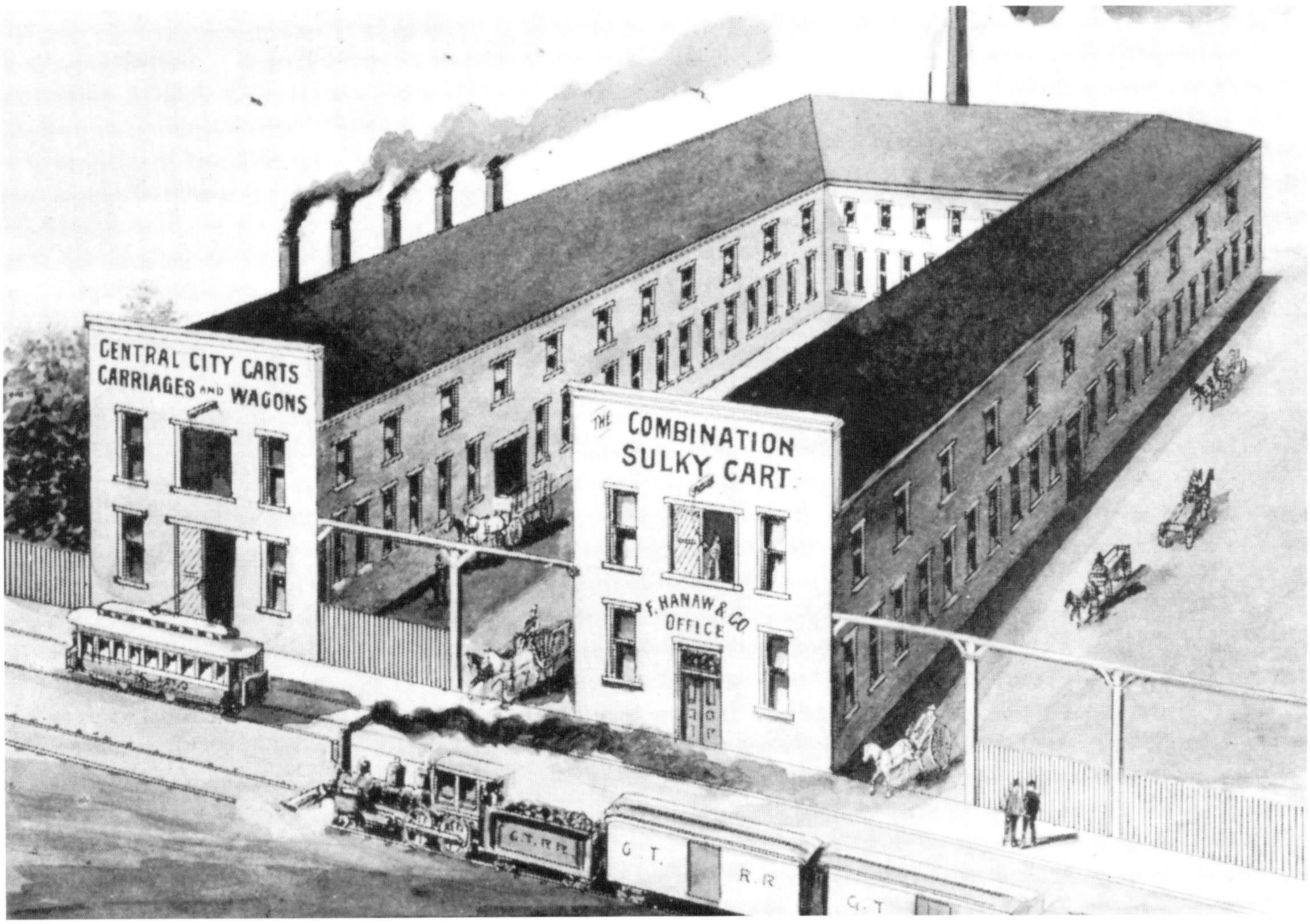

Ferdinand Hanaw's carriage company made the small, two-wheeled 'Combination Speeder' sulky cart. Hanaw's company was typical of carriage factories founded in Jackson after 1890. Unlike the small, handicraft carriage shops, Hanaw's carriage designs were standardized and heavy investments were made in machinery for the production of standard parts.

Jackson's longest-lasting wagon and carriage company was undoubtedly the Austin, Tomlinson and Webster Company, makers of the Jackson prison wagon. The wagon-builder began in 1837, as a modest shop run by Joseph Beebe, employing contracted prison labor. The company changed hands several times, becoming Austin, Tomlinson and Webster in 1859 when E.A. Webster joined the company.

Webster brought many new ideas to the wagonmaker, including advertising. One Webster ad campaign distributed hundreds of painted, cast-iron frogs adorned with the words "I Croak For The Jackson Wagon." Others, such as Colonel Ed Hogan's balloon lifts of Jackson Wagons into the area's skies, were more spectacular.

Advertising aside, the company achieved notoriety for its products. In 1887, Austin, Tomlinson and Webster directors received a letter from none other than P.T. Barnum. The note was filled with praise for the company's wagon which Barnum used to move his elephant, 'Jumbo,' through the streets of London. The wagons gained some small fame worldwide and by the turn of the century, the company was producing over 6,000 wagons per year.

An 1895 engraving depicting the Austin, Tomlinson and Webster factory.

Colonel Edward Hogan, a Jackson regular during the latter nineteenth century, hoists a Jackson Wagon aloft.

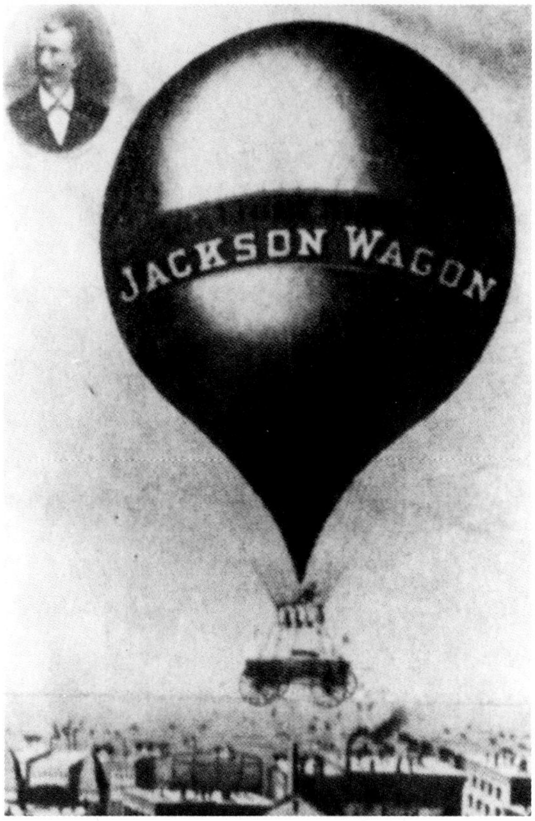

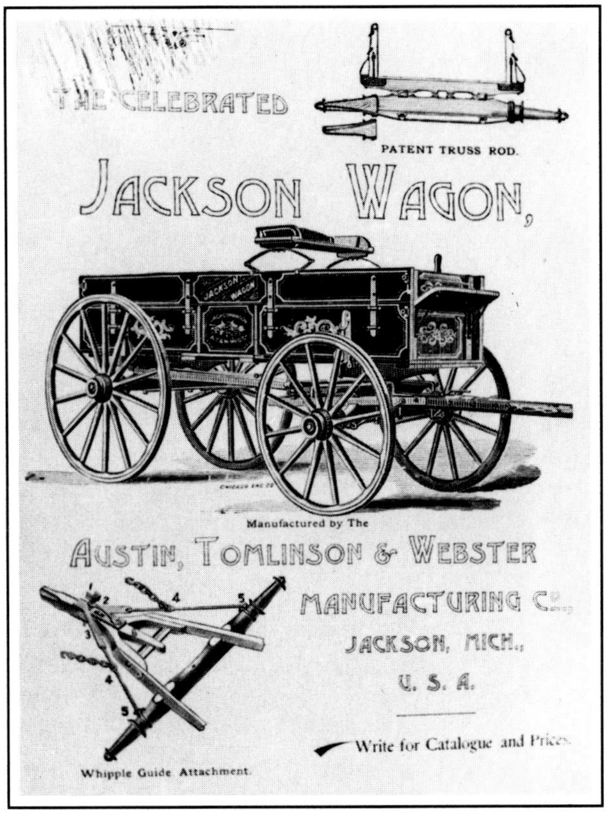

A nineteenth century Jackson Wagon advertisement.

This "Wait For The Wagon" sheet music was distributed, for a time, with all purchases of Austin, Tomlinson and Webster vehicles. The man appearing in the center of the wagon's wheel is Edward A. Webster.

Henry H. Smith

The 1889 'Citizen Industrial Edition' carried this illustration of the 'Collins Cart.' The makers of the 'Collins Cart' produced over 15,000 vehicles every year after 1895 and continued to do a thriving business until the early 1900s, when the automobile slowly replaced horse-drawn vehicles.

The Collins Manufacturing Company and its nineteenth century 'Collins Cart' were well-known pieces of Jackson's nineteenth century scenery. The factory, built in 1895, still stands in Jackson today as the Commercial Exchange Building.

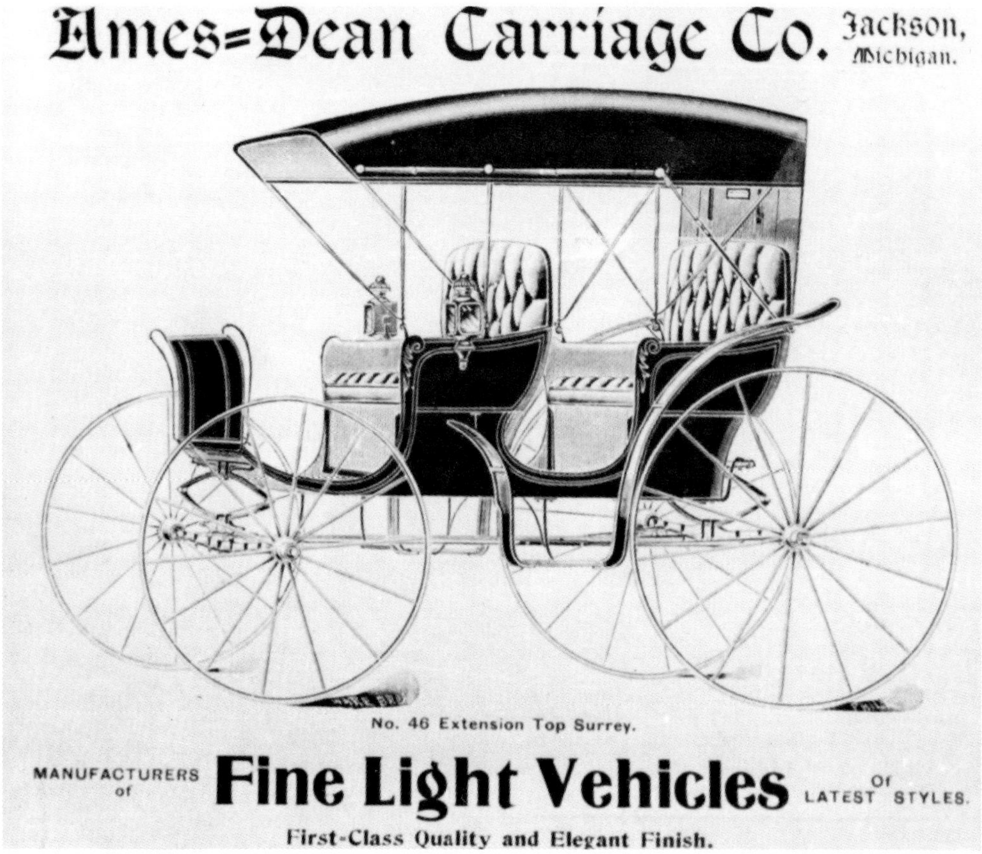

The Ames-Dean Carriage Company built its first horse-drawn vehicle in 1897 and built its last gasoline-powered car in 1910. Like several other of Jackson's large wagon and carriage makers, Ames-Dean attempted to adjust to the rise of the automobile, but without success.

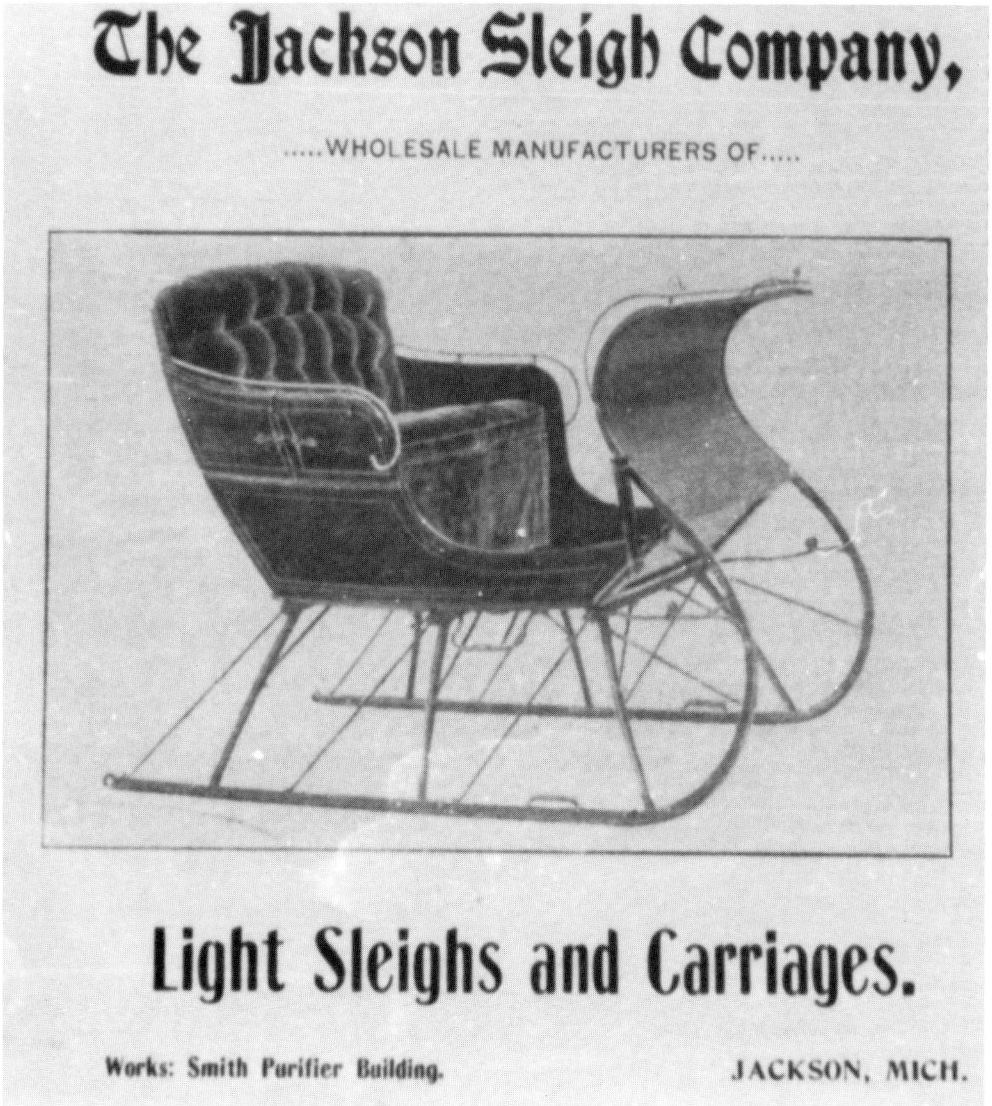

An advertisement for the Jackson Sleigh Company.

FROM CARRIAGES TO CARS

Jackson and the Automobile

Automobiles were still rare and exotic contraptions in the few years before the turn of the twentieth century: the first American-made car was sold in 1893 and six years later there were an estimated 3,000 automobiles in the country. Horse-drawn carriages were everyman's transportation. In the 1890s, motorcars were the interests of tinkering machinists, bicycle shop owners and wealthy businessmen. Only visionaries could guess that within fifteen years the automobile would become a major part of American life.

Five years into the new century, the horse and carriage were on their way out as the most popular form of transportation and eager mechanics in machine shops nationwide were mounting gasoline-powered engines onto carriages, buggies and bicycles. Jackson —like Detroit, Dearborn and Flint — was home to its share of dreaming, experimental carmakers.

One Jackson innovator, Coe S. Reeves, built his first gasoline-powered vehicle in 1897. The owner of a small, Jackson bicycle shop, Reeves put his spare time to work in building a three-wheeled runabout that resembled a tricycle with an engine. Others, like Byron J. Carter and Arthur Butcher, built similar, highly experimental 'cars.' And within a few short years, automobilemaking in Jackson grew from a skilled

Coe S. Reeves created this three-wheeled runabout, resembling a tricycle with a gasoline motor attached. Reeves, owner of a small bicycle shop at 157 West Pearl Street, built the experimental car in 1897. Reeves never went into any serious automobile production, but his experimental was, nevertheless, influential.

This 1903 steam-powered experimental was one of two built by Butcher and Gage — owners of a Jackson automobile repair and storage business. The small firm never went into actual vehicle production themselves; instead, they began manufacturing automobile parts for Jackson's local carmakers.

Fred Lockwood, accompanied by his wife, Lydia, drives one of the Lockwood Brothers' experimental vehicles on one of early Jackson's narrow, unpaved roads.

machinist's hobby to a widespread industrial pursuit.

In 1902, six years before the introduction of Henry Ford's famous Model T, several Jackson entrepreneurs had gathered to form the Jackson Automobile Company — makers of the Jackson car. The Jackson Automobile Company was the city's first successful, long-lived auto-maker. In 1910, nearly 1,000 men were working for the city's car manufacturers and almost 500 of them were Jackson Automobile Company employees. But even with 500 workers, the company only made about 14 cars per day.

By 1910, Michigan's auto producers had grown highly competitive and makers in Detroit, Flint and Dearborn — backed by huge capital investments — were manufacturing more cars at less expense. Auto prices plummeted nationwide with the introduction of moving assembly lines, precision standard parts and other mass-production innovations. By contrast, most of Jackson's automobile producers concentrated their attention on large, luxurious and somewhat expensive cars. The 1923 opening of Henry Ford's gigantic River Rouge factory conveniently marks the year when the mass market triumphed: no early Jackson auto-maker lasted beyond 1924. Of Jackson's auto companies, only the Briscoe Motor Corporation successfully adopted Detroit auto-makers' mass-production techniques. Briscoe made over 48,000 cars between 1914 and 1922: one of every two cars ever made in Jackson was a Briscoe.

Jackson's carmakers produced twenty-one different makes during the city's twenty years in the motor vehicle business. Cars like the Earl or the Ames-Dean sound unfamiliar today, but they were foundations for Jackson's heavy industrial manufacturing. What is more, they helped to change forever the way Jacksonians saw themselves and their city.

CARS MADE IN JACKSON

Ames	1901 - 1905
Argo	1914 - 1915
Briscoe	1914 - 1921
Buick	1905 - 1912
C.V.I.	1907 - 1908
Carter	- 1905
Cutting	1910 - 1913
Duck	- 1913
Earl	1921 - 1924
Fuller	1907 - 1910
Globe	- 1907
Hackett	1916 - 1919
Hollier	1915 - 1921
Imperial	1908 - 1916
Jackson	1903 - 1923
Jaxon	1902 - 1904
Kaiser-Darrin	- 1954
Marion-Handley	1916 - 1920
Orlo	- 1904
Standard Electric	1912 - 1915
Steel Swallow	1907 - 1908

Jacksonians, like most Americans of the period, were fascinated with the 'horseless carriage.' Many of the city's new companies began producing automobiles in the early 1900s while Jackson's carriage and cart makers began to decline with the car's growing popularity. Realizing that horse-drawn vehicles were becoming a thing of the past, the directors of two Jackson 'carriage works' made attempts to motorize their products. The Ames-Dean Company and the Fuller Buggy Company created vehicles that were essentially carriages or buggies with gasoline motors attached. But both the Ames and the Fuller failed to make it as cars. Ames-Dean made only three prototypes and Fuller, though more successful than Ames-Dean, ceased manufacturing cars after merely three years.

The Fuller Buggy Company's factory as it appeared in 1895. Carriages, carts and light wagons were made by the thousands in the Fuller factory, and the company unsuccessfully attempted to adjust to the new auto industry in the late 1900s. Fuller's president, George A. Matthews, later became one of the principal figures in the Jackson Automobile Company.

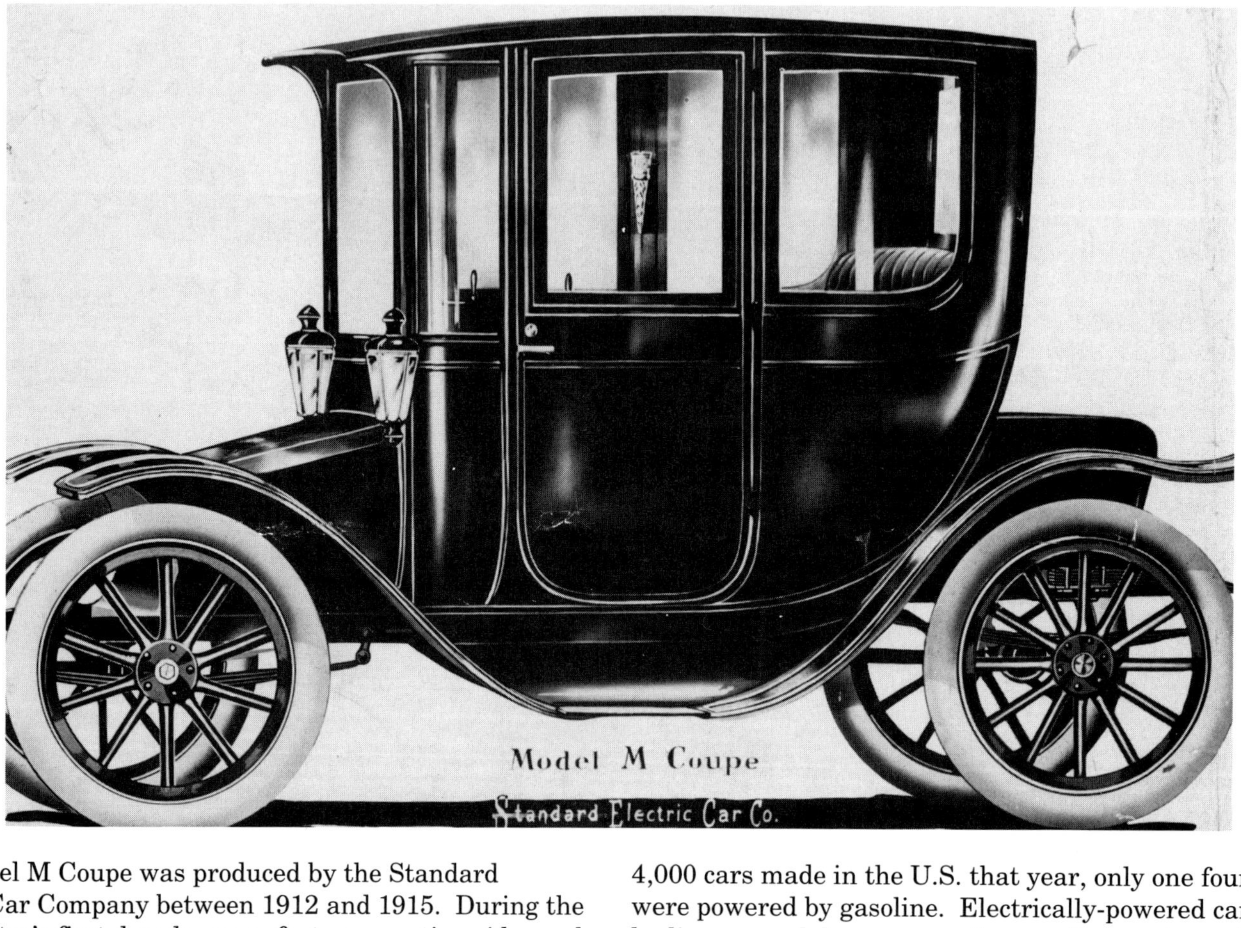

This Model M Coupe was produced by the Standard Electric Car Company between 1912 and 1915. During the car industry's first decade, manufacturers nationwide used electrically-powered engines in their designs. In fact, steam and electrical power were favored over gasoline engines in many early cars. In 1900, of the approximately 4,000 cars made in the U.S. that year, only one fourth were powered by gasoline. Electrically-powered cars slowly disappeared, however, as the gasoline engine gained prominence for its power and durability. Although the Standard Electric was billed as "The Car That Excels, The Car That Outsells," the company disbanded in 1915.

The director of Flint's Durant-Dort Carriage Company, W.C. Durant, helped David Buick's struggling young car company to its feet in late 1904. Buick needed money and factory space and Durant provided both, moving Buick production to an idle Durant-Dort company plant in Jackson. By 1905, the newly equipped factory was ready and nearly 1,000 Model C Buicks were made there that year.

William Crapo Durant

Buick's cars quickly became popular, and Durant began seeking capital for the company's expansion. He found the needed money, but not in Jackson. Agreements were made, in 1906, between Durant and Flint political leaders that resulted in Buick's move back to Flint in 1907. Production of the Buick Model F continued in Jackson through 1908 and Buick trucks were made in the city as late as 1912.

THE JACKSON

This 1903 advertisement proclaimed the advantages of the "Jaxon" automobile. Its producer, the Jackson Automobile Company, was formed in 1902 by Byron J. Carter and local business owners George Matthews and Charles Lewis. Less than six years later, the company became one of Jackson's largest employers.

Portrait of B.J. Carter

The steam-run "Jaxon" soon became the "Jackson" gasoline-powered car. This photograph, showing a "Jackson" being driven around the company's test track, was taken in 1908. Company employees tested each "Jackson" for possible mechanical problems before the finished body work was added. A "Jackson" similar to the one shown here, proved itself on an even larger test track in 1909: a Model "E," driven by Jacksonian Leigh Lynch, won the Indianapolis Motor Speedway's Wheeler-Schebler cup. Lynch and the Jackson Automobile Company took home $10,000 after beating 18 contenders in a 300-mile race.

By 1915, the Jackson Automobile Company commanded a network of car dealers and distributors. Here, a group of car dealers return to the company's East Michigan Avenue plant after a 1915 promotional tour of northern Michigan's rugged roads.

Advertisements for "Jackson" cars carried the slogan "No Hill Too Steep, No Sand Too Deep."

These Jacksons were photographed at the 1906 New York Auto Show at the Grand Central Palace.

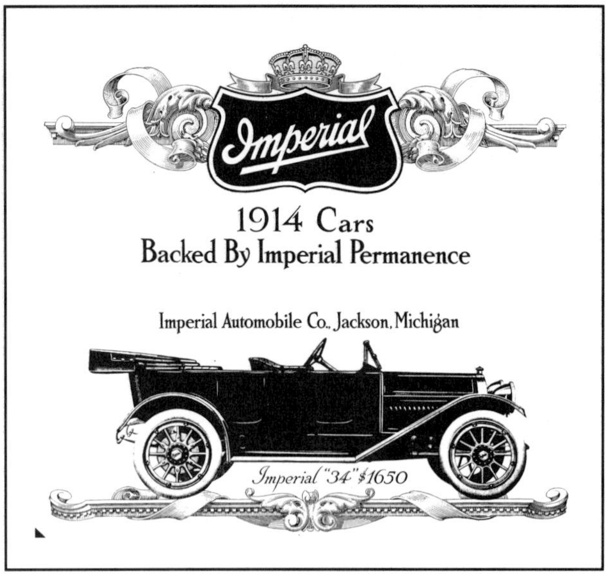

THE IMPERIAL

The Imperial Automobile Company joined Jackson's thriving new car industry in 1908 and remained in production until early 1916. Around 300 Imperial cars were made the first year and new, incoming orders for the next model year were close to one thousand. The initial success of the 'Imperial' and the demand that it seemed to bring on from the public pushed the company's officers to expand their manufacturing capability. Imperial Auto moved into part of the old Durant-Dort carriage plant at Ganson and Wisner, vacated by Buick in 1912.

The 'Imperial' was successfully produced for three years at the Wisner Street plant, but in 1915, a portion of the factory was being prepared for the Marion Motor Company. By 1916, Imperial Auto and Marion Motor had merged to form the Mutual Motors Company. J.L. Handley became the president of the new motor car company and the product's nameplate was changed to 'Marion-Handley.'

'Marion-Handley' automobiles were produced one at a time, in the old style, at stationary work areas. Parts were brought by laborers to mechanics, who then assembled the car from the ground up. Use of moving assembly lines by rival companies both in Jackson and in Michigan's other car producing cities became much more prevalent after 1914. Mutual Motors never adopted such a specialized, moving assembly system as did the more successful makers of the 'Briscoe' and 'Jackson' cars, and it is very possible that this helped speed the company's demise. 'Marion-Handley' production ceased after 1919.

J.L. Handley,
president of the Mutual Motors Company.

A group of Mutual Motors Company employees as they appeared while waiting to ring in on the time clock, ca. 1918.

MARION HANDLEY

This advertisement for the 'Marion-Handley' appeared in the April, 1917, edition of Motor Magazine.

Draftsmen at work in their Mutual Motors Company studio, ca. 1918.

MARION-HANDLEY

W.W. Wellington, production manager for the Mutual Motors Company, and his secretary, ca. 1915. Note the 'Imperial' advertisement pinned to the wall behind Mr. Wellington.

Jackson Chamber of Commerce members inspect the final assembly area of the 'Marion-Handley'.

A view of the Mutual Motors Company facility at Wisner and Ganson streets, ca. 1915.

Two spare tires? Early road conditions were crude and flats were commonplace. The Marion-Handley's trunk was designed to hold several spares. Note the car's exposed gas tank.

ARGO

An advertisement, ca. 1915, for the Argo automobile.

The New York-based Argo Motor Co. came to Jackson late in 1913. Benjamin Briscoe, made arrangements to produce the Argo in the city while making preparations for the much larger Briscoe Motors Corporation. Argo was eventually absorbed by Briscoe Motors in 1915 and the facilities for producing the small, brisk two-seater were sold to Mansell Hackett one year later.

BRISCOE

Jackson's first taste of today's 'industrial' assembly came with the Briscoe automobile. Of Jackson's auto companies, only the Briscoe Motor Corporation successfully adopted mass-production and moving assembly line techniques. In its seven years of existence the company drove nearly 50,000 Briscoe and Earl automobiles out of the assembly rooms. Other Jackson carmakers were using the older methods of stationary work areas in which entire cars were built from the wheels up. Briscoe's use of a moving assembly line, where workers concentrated on a single, specialized and repetitive task, increased the company's output beyond its local competitors. Like Henry Ford's large Highland Park and River Rouge plants, Jackson's Briscoe factories were filled with workers standing in place as parts moved before them.

Briscoe advertisement taken from a 1920 edition of *Literary Digest* magazine.

Benjamin Briscoe

Workers drive almost-finished Briscoe cars off of the moving assembly line's end, ca. 1921.

Briscoe's Industrial Workers

The constant increase in the size of Jackson's automobile companies was accompanied by larger office staffs. Here, Briscoe Motors employees work in the company's printing and communications office. Note the differences between today's computer technologies and the older, mechanical devices used in 1920.

Before the advent of the computer, invoices, records and accounting were all done by hand. Note the machine being used by the woman at the desk second from left, center. It was known as a 'Comptometer,' and was a bulky, mechanical version of today's silicon chip calculator.

Women at work. These sewing machine operators finished the leather upholstery and 'top-work' used in the Briscoe automobiles. Patterning, cutting, sewing, stuffing and polishing were all done by hand in this department.

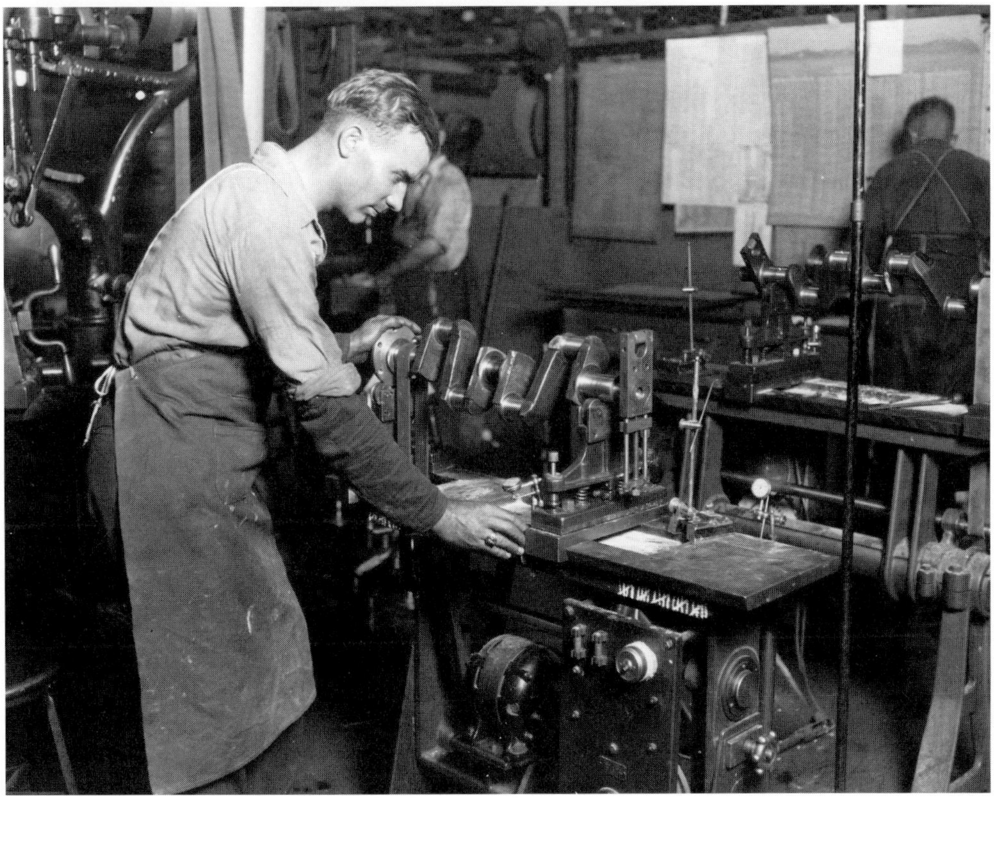

Not all of Briscoe's machine and metal workers were stationed on moving assembly lines: employees, such as those pictured here, sometimes worked at stationary work areas to produce parts that would later be dropped into a frame.

A Briscoe employee performing a tolerance test on a Briscoe camshaft. Tolerance tests indicated how close the camshaft was to the desired standard size: parts that were too large or too small disrupted the motor's operation and were discarded. Note chalk marks on the base of this machine that indicate how many camshafts he has inspected.

DOUBLE 3

The working conditions of the fully mechanized industrial age presented new dangers to the worker: high noise levels, spinning belts, self-moving cutting tools and heavy racks and bins made being alert very important. Here, workers attend machines producing gear blanks for Briscoe transmissions.

Early assembly lines were often a series of gravity slides and roller lines such as the one pictured here. When an employee finished his or her operation, the part was pushed along the rollers to the next employee. Later, such lines were mechanized.

Briscoe, like Ford Motor Co. and other Detroit automakers, invested heavily in labor-saving machinery. This drill press simultaneously performed over twenty drilling operations—a task that formerly had been done one hole at a time.

Briscoe finished large quantities of similar, precision parts for use on a moving assembly line: here, workers finish body fenders in preparation for final assembly.

The main Briscoe Motors assembly line was over 500 feet long and used a chain drive to pull the frame of the car being built. Such moving lines are commonplace in almost every industry today, but during the days of Jackson's auto manufacturing, they were strikingly new innovations.

Car makers were eager to point out that automobiles were as easily operated by women as they were by men. Here, a woman poses for a photographer in a new 1921 Earl.

THE EARL

Clarence Earl

A 1923 Earl automobile, parked in front of a Jackson home.

A view of the interior of a 1922 Earl car shows the vast differences between yesterday's and today's automobile. Note the rear-seat heater, built into the floor.

A shot of an Earl touring sedan as seen from the rear.

A woman daintily demonstrates entry into the rear seat of a two-door Earl sedan.

CORSETS

Jackson Corset Company's style No. 155 as it appeared in the early 1920s.

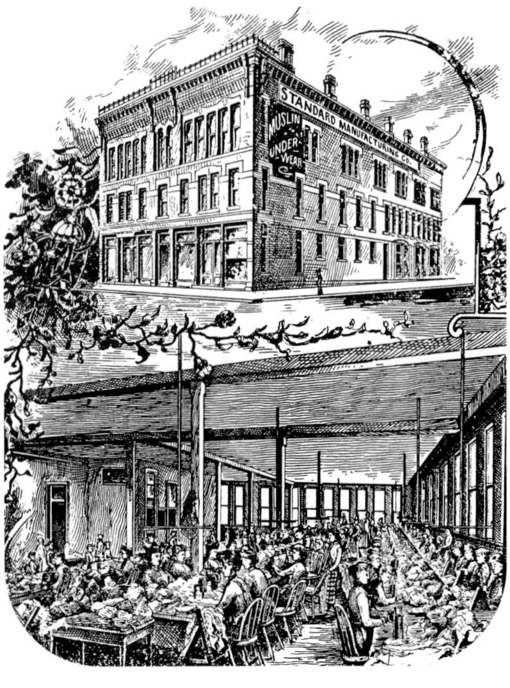

This illustration depicting the Standard Manufacturing Company appeared alongside an article in Jackson's 1889 *Citizen Industrial Edition* newspaper. Standard Manufacturing was organized in 1882 and quickly grew to be the second largest corset manufacturer in the city and one of its largest employers of young women. "Over fifty families have come to this city during the past three years to enable their daughters to get employment at this great factory," the article boasted. "Once mastering the trade an industrious girl can make from $7 to $10 per week. It is not infrequent that the daughter has a larger weekly stipend than her father..."

This advertisement for the Coronet Corset Company's 'Flexibone' model appeared in the September, 1895 edition of *The Ladies' Home Journal*.

Today's reader may not be familiar with the nineteenth century's corset, a laced or hooked undergarment that was worn beneath women's clothing. The corset was reinforced with steel or whalebone, and tightening it constricted a woman's body, forcing it to conform to fashionable, thin-waisted styles. Production of such undergarments became a major Jackson industry in the late 1870s when M.K. Bortree's patented 'Duplex Corset' gained popularity in eastern marketplaces.

Moses Bortree, a Pennsylvania native who had migrated to Michigan in 1866, moved to Jackson and founded a hoop skirt factory in 1868. With his invention of the Duplex Corset in 1875, Bortree expanded his facilities and within five years production rose from 50,000 to 300,000 corsets per year. The growing firm attracted the attention of some of early Jackson's wealthiest businessmen, including P.B. Loomis and Edward Webster, who purchased company stock. The continued growth of Bortree's corset factory helped to attract laborers to the community. The manufacturer employed almost 400 people, 350 of whom were women.

By 1895, Jackson was home to six large corset manufacturers. One of these, the Coronet Corset Manufactory, was unique for its female president and director, Mrs. C.A. McGee: women in such positions were a nineteenth century rarity. McGee designed and patented her 'Cornet Corset,' and began its production in 1880. Her company eventually became one of Jackson's most successful.

By the latter years of the nineteenth century, women working outside the home had become fairly common to America's growing industrial cities and in 1892, Michigan's Bureau of Labor and Industrial Statistics investigated the working conditions of female laborers in such cities throughout Michigan. The Bureau's report showed that Jackson's undergarment factory employees were predominantly women, ranging in age from 12 to 50 years, and that on average they worked almost 65 hours per week. Women corset-makers were paid from $0.40 to $1.30 per day. Though this was roughly half of what men performing comparable tasks were paid, the Bureau claimed that women workers in Jackson were among the highest paid in the state. Work in Jackson's corset companies continued to grow in popularity as a source of female employment.

By 1910, almost one fifth of Jackson's industrial workers were female operatives working in six different corset companies and the city had become one of the United States' corset production giants. Jackson was home to such factories as the Reliance Corset Company, the Jackson Skirt and Novelty Company and the American Lady Corset Company, among others. These garment makers ran some of the largest production facilities in Jackson, with each factory typically employing several hundred women and men.

Most of Jackson's big corset makers have long since disappeared. After 1920, increasing competition from eastern makers and changing women's fashions caused almost all of Jackson's corset and undergarment factories to close or sell. Exceptions were the S. H. Camp Company, Kellogg Corset and the I. M. Dach Company. All three continued to thrive after the passing of corset-making's heyday.

These women modeled the Jackson Corset Company's various products for advertisements. Corset styles changed over the years for pragmatic reasons as much as for change in fashion design. As women became increasingly involved in the work outside of the home, the corset's restriction of free movement grew very impractical. Late nineteenth and early twentieth century dress reform movements in the U.S. pushed for the elimination of the corset. As one Jackson corset factory worker told Michigan's Labor Bureau in 1892, "I know from extensive observation that the wearing of corsets is very injurious to the health of women...The principal motive [of the dress reform movement] is undoubtedly a worthy one, namely, to give greater freedom of motion to women, to dispense with the health-breaking corset and to shift the weight of clothing from the waist, where it now is, to the shoulders, where it ought to be."

A model displays a Camp undergarment. In addition to corsets, the Camp Company began producing medical supports and prosthetic aids after World War II.

Samuel H. Camp

The S.H. Camp Company was founded in 1908 and throughout its history in Jackson, the company has moved to several locations. After a fire destroyed Camp's facilities in 1927, the company moved to the building pictured here, former home of the American Lady Corset Company.

The sales staff of the S.H. Camp Company posed outside of the company's downtown Jackson Goodwin Shop. The Goodwin Corset was Camp's leading seller during the company's early years. S.H. Camp is seated in the front row with his wife, Margaret, seated to his right.

Organized in 1899, the principal garment of the Jackson Shirt and Novelty Company was the "Elite" petticoat. The company claimed the Elite to be "the first successfully fitted top petticoat to be put on the market."

The Jackson Corset Company's factory, as it appeared ca. 1915, where many dozens of corsets were made every day. Note the employees sitting on the lawn. The company maintained an extensive garden in which employees ate their lunch or took an afternoon stroll. More workers peer from the second and third-story factory windows.

The stripping, folding and cutting room: here, bulk cloth was un-wound from the bolt and layered in preparation for the cutting process.

The Jackson Corset Company's cutting room, where workers handcut patterned pieces from the layered piles of folded cloth.

The cutting room of the Kellogg Corset Company.

The main operating rooms of the Kellogg Corset Company, where various stripping, sewing and pressing procedures were performed.

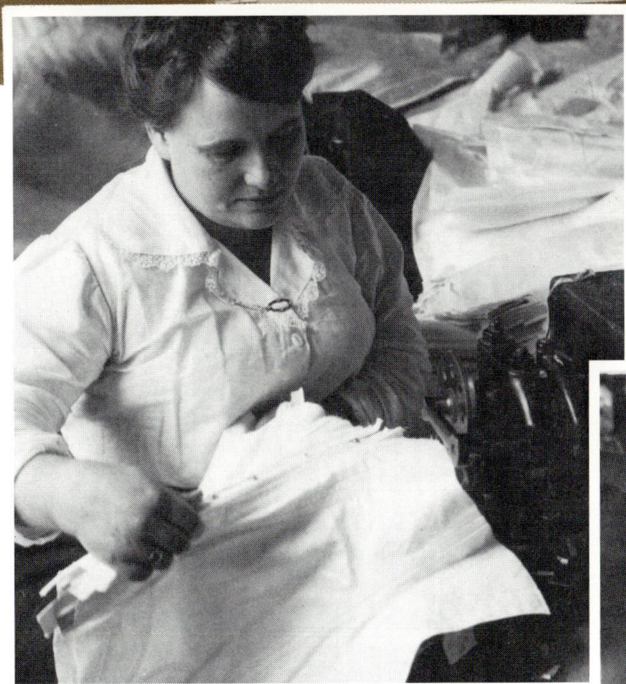

Here, a Jackson Corset Company worker uses a shaping machine to form the top and bottom line of the corset. The machine produced a finished edge, pressing the frayed edges in preparation for sewing.

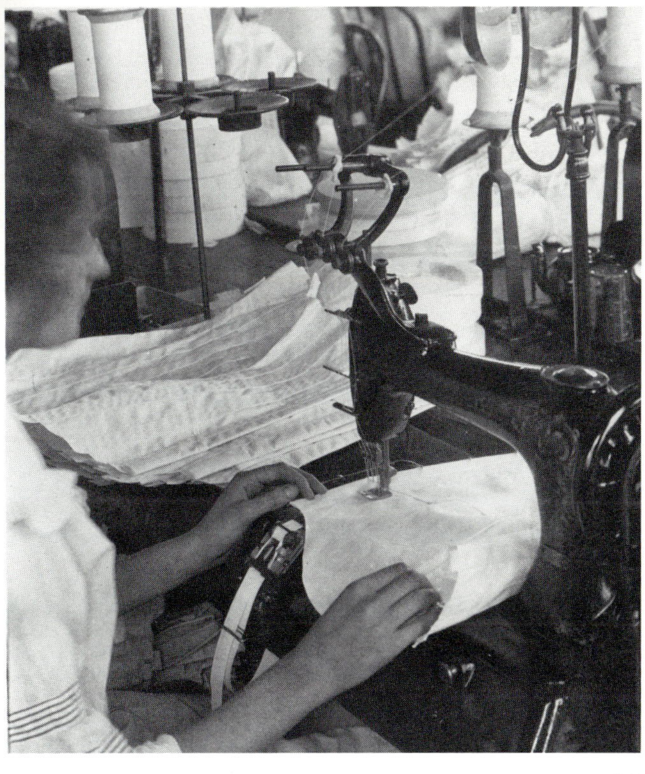

This woman, operating a 'three-needle stripping machine', was one of fifty performing the same task at the Jackson Corset Company. The machine attached a reinforcing 'strip' of cloth to the corset lining.

A view of the north operating room of the Jackson Corset Company. The long tables in the room were arranged like an assembly line, with the employees performing specialized operations to make almost 500 corsets every working day.

This 'eyeleting machine' consumed an entire barrel of tiny, metal rings every operating day. The machine took over one of the corset-makers' most skilled, but tedious, tasks, and completely attached 22 reinforcing 'eyelets' to the corset in a single operation.

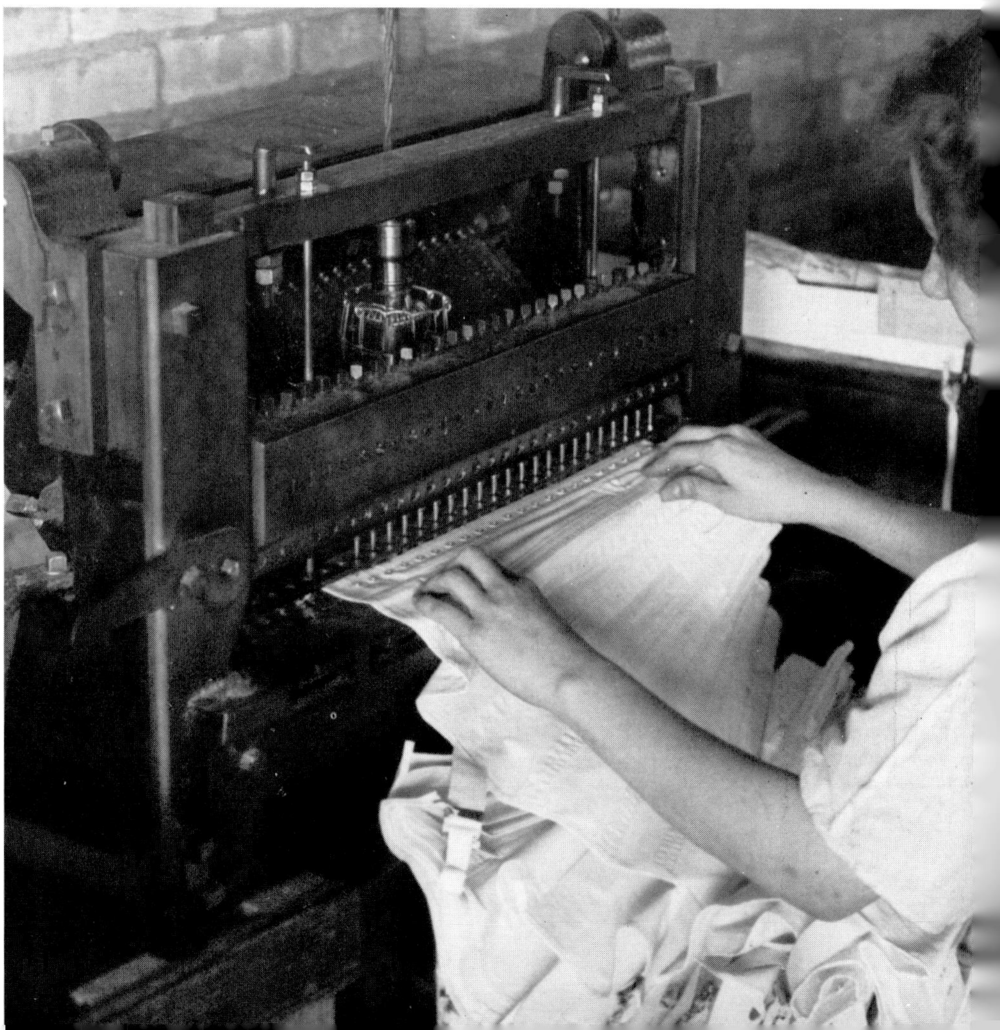

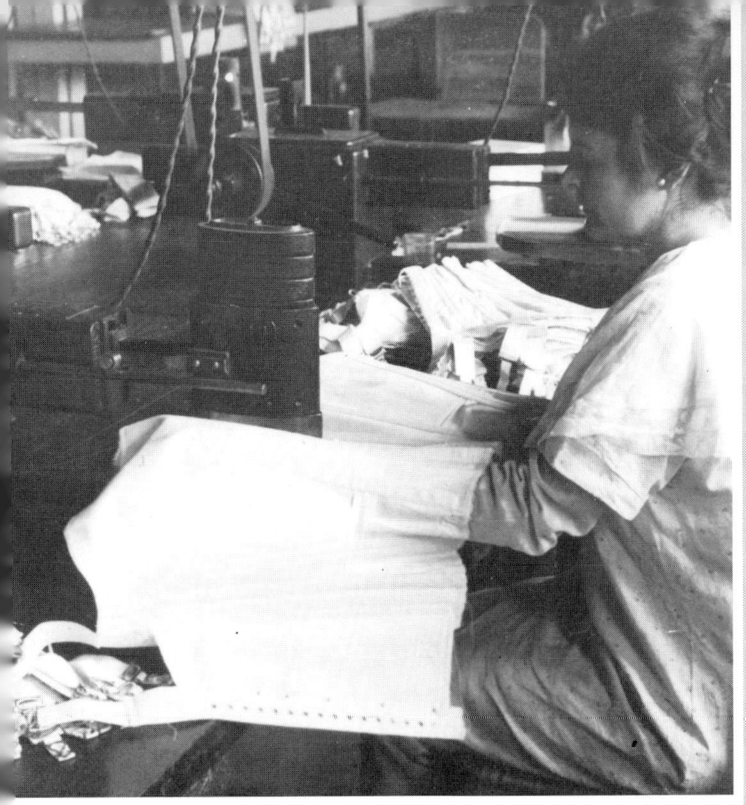

An electric ironing machine was used in one of the corset-finishing operations, in preparation for shipping.

A view of the examining room where each corset was inspected before being boxed for storage or shipping.

The Jackson Corset Company made its own packaging materials. This view shows the box-making department, where six thousand labeled packages were made each day.

H.H. Stiles, president of the Jackson Corset Company, ca. 1918.

The office of C.H. Tompkins, vice-president of the Jackson Corset Company. The management of the Jackson Corset Company ran an extensive sales network: as early as 1895, Jackson Corset Company salesmen were traveling throughout the U.S. and to other countries as well.

Expansion of the Jackson Corset Company's production included management expansions in the advertising and sales departments. This view shows the advertising room, where various promotionals for the company's 'JCC' and 'College Girl' corsets were produced.

Jackson's women corset-makers often formed tightly-knit social groups. The J.C.C. Club, made up of Jackson Corset Company employees, held dinners and social events. Pictured here are J.C.C. Club members as they appeared in 1912, preparing to sit down to a special banquet.

A view of the lunch and break room of the Jackson Corset Company, where employees talked, sang and socialized.

Interior of the Crowley operation.

Crowley Boiler Company

One of the more unusual companies operating in Jackson was the Crowley Boiler Company. As the photos indicate they built huge boilers for manufacturing firms, schools, etc.

The following is from an early newspaper clipping concerning the photo on the top right but could certainly apply to the photo below as well. The picture was taken while two huge steel tanks for the American Radiator Co. of Detroit were enroute to Detroit. *The tanks were constructed by the John Crowley Boiler Co. of Jackson, and being too large to load on to a car were placed on sledges and started overland for Detroit, the journey commencing on*

Monday. The tanks are 12 feet wide and 12 feet high, weigh several tons, and tested at 150 pounds steam pressure. Their width made it impossible to ship them by rail, as they would extend so far beyond the width of the cars as to interfere with traffic on the double tracks. Two teams of horses were sent to Jackson by the Radiator Co. to haul the tanks to this city.

Many times before Grass Lake was reached, the Detroit horses became stalled on the road, and it was finally found necessary to turn the job over to the Union Truck Co. of Jackson. Two teams of the largest draft horses in Jackson were substituted for the Detroit teams, and the procession forged on over the snowy roads and through the intense cold for this city, where it is expected they will arrive tomorrow if they make schedule time.

Foundries and Machines

Manufacturing methods in the United States changed significantly after the close of the Civil War. During the 1860s and '70s, the small, traditional shops of skilled craftsmen were replaced, more and more often, by larger 'manufactories.' These new manufactories were different from their predecessors in many ways, but the most significant change was in their use of machines to produce large volumes of products.

They also began using standard parts and product designs to make mass production more feasible. Instead of one man working on a single product, from 'start to finish,' the new 'manufactories' used machines to perform the different steps in the 'start to finish' process.

In the 1860s, companies in Jackson began to make standardized lines of products, too. Many of them required specialized machines to do shaping, cutting or molding that had previously been done by hand. The considerable local importance of flour-milling equipment and machinery manufacturing increased the demand for local foundries and blacksmith's skills. Even more influential was the increased expansion of the railroad in the 1870s and the re-location of the Michigan Central Railroad's locomotive repair and manufacturing shops from Marshall to Jackson in 1871. The 1860s and 1870s witnessed widespread move from water to steam power in manufacturing and the availability of cheap, locally mined coal made steam power very popular with Jackson industrialists. Use of the new

Two views of the Holton and Weatherwax Foundry and Machine Shop, ca. 1895. Holton and Weatherwax supplied many of the local corset-making companies with 'corset steels:' the steel reinforcements that were sewn into the corset to make it stiff. The foundry did other types of business as well. It was a large 'manufactory' for its day, employing over one hundred people.

steam technology created a demand for machinists.

Small blacksmithing shops and foundries were a part of Jackson from its very beginning: but after 1870, more and more foundries, machine shops and blacksmithing services opened and serviced the growing demands of Jackson's manufacturers. Many of the city's manufacturers wanted special machinery to do tasks that had once been performed by individual craftsmen. Those shops which already existed, such as the Vandercook Brothers and Lusk Foundry and Machine Shop (founded in 1853) expanded their facilities and specialized their services. Jackson's foundries and machine shops also began the production of steam engines and specialty metal-forming tools. The Jackson Foundry and Machine Co., the E.Dennis and Co. Machine Manufactory, The Bennett Machine Co. Foundry and Machine Shop and the Bolinger Manufacturing Company were just a few of Jackson's earliest industrial machine-makers.

For a time, the fantastic growth of metal manufacturing and machine-making in Jackson prompted a few of the city's wealthiest business owners to invest in an iron ore refining operation. In 1872, the Jackson Rolling Mills were built and the Rolling Mills' backers hoped that Jackson would become a major ore refining center. Operating expenses proved too high, however, and the demand too low: the Rolling Mills were closed and though Jackson's metal-working industries continued to grow, the city never became a 'refining town.'

The E. Dennis And Company Machine Manufactory was one of Jackson's oldest. Elmore Dennis established his business in 1872 and produced much of the machinery used by George T. Smith to manufacture his flour-purifier machines. A description listed their 'concern' as "job work in machinery, making a specialty of pullies, shaftings and couplings...[and] a large amount of woodworking machinery."

The use of steam engines required large, sturdy, iron boilers. The Keeley and Crowley Jackson City Boiler Works made a specialty of such products.

Withington-Cooley Company

One of the earliest of these small metal-working 'manufactories' had its beginning at the Michigan State Prison in 1847, when several Ohio businessmen signed contracts with warden John Titus for the labor of over one hundred prisoners. According to the original contract, the Pinney-Connable Company's convict laborers were involved in making 'woolen and cotton goods, carpeting, farming tools generally, saddle trees and trimmings, hames and harness trimmings, steam engines and boilers, barrels and copper ware.' The first steam engine to be used in a Jackson business was produced by Pinney-Connable's convict laborers.

It wasn't long before the Pinney-Connable Company turned its attention solely to making metal hand tools and agricultural equipment. In 1858 the firm was sold to new owners, William Withington and Harold Sprague. By the 1870s, the name Withington-Cooley Company had been adopted — but that was hardly the extent of the change. The farm toolsmaker had vastly expanded their facilities: in 1870, the company employed over 200 men, including 140 convicts on contract labor. Mass production techniques, machinery and shipping of products outside of the city by rail had become routine parts of their business.

William H. Withington

Workers began to concentrate on one specific part or task within the whole set of production steps and the Withington-Cooley Company began turning out products numbering in the thousands. "They are continually adding to their capital and manufacturing facilities," an admiring Jacksonian wrote in 1869, "The order and system which pervades all departments of labor required to produce the manifold articles in their large list is admirable...They have three main shops...with bending, grinding, painting, boiler and engine room in addition...There is a room entirely devoted to polishing with emery."

By 1880, the Withington-Cooley Company became one of nineteenth century Jackson's largest manufacturers of metal products and they were the largest contractor with the state prison for convict labor. Their products were shipped all over the United States and to other countries, as well. Following the death of William Withington in 1903, the Withington-Cooley Company was merged with the American Fork and Hoe Company of Cleveland. The company remained the largest producer of agricultural implements in the city of Jackson and continued using contracted convict labor through 1912.

An engraving depicting the exterior of the Withington-Cooley Company's factory.

Advertisements for Withington-Cooley farm tools.

The American Fork And Hoe Building, ca. 1925.

This photo, ca. 1910, was taken in front of the Lusk foundries, one of Jackson's oldest. Seated fourth from left is George Lusk, the foundry's owner. Lusk foundry was later changed to the Pioneer Foundry.

The George D. Walcott & Sons Company was founded in 1881 at 414 North Jackson Street and it was one of Jackson's first and most successful machine tools makers. The company specialized in machines for the shaping and cutting of metal, such as the Walcott Shaping Machine pictured here, described as "especially adapted for railroad work." The Walcott Company supplied Jackson's manufacturers with 'machines for making machines.' Below is a photograph of its North Jackson Street plant as it appeared in the early 1920s.

Express and Package Services

The growth of large industry and commerce in Jackson created many new demands and opportunities for small businesses. Before the days of large, national package delivery companies, most cities and towns had local 'express'or 'dray' companies that specialized in delivering packages and products, much as the mail does today. Jackson was home to many such small companies, many of them run by a single person whose stock consisted of nothing more than a horse and a heavy duty wagon, or 'dray.'

This interior shot of the Wells, Abbey and Wells warehouse shows the variety of objects which Jackson's express companies delivered throughout the city and county.

One of Jackson's express services was Wells, Abbey and Wells. The company employed roughly twenty people—movers, loaders, warehouse keepers, drivers and deliverers. This photograph was taken in 1915. A partial view of the horse-drawn wagons used to deliver goods can be seen in the background.

Breweries, Beer, & Pubs

Saloons and bars had become a familiar sight along Jackson's busy streets by the turn of the century. In 1870 there were almost 25 saloons in the city and by 1885 the number had almost tripled. Both workers and employers were known to frequent such popular socializing spots to enjoy the several available local brews.

Jackson was home to many small brewers and bottlers in the 1870s and 1880s, among them Gottlieb Frey and Thomas Mills. Frey practiced his craft at the Jackson Brewery for over a decade, opening a business around 1872. He later sold it to Carl Eberle in 1886. Purney and Co. supplied local pubs but kept their operation on a small scale. Two of Jackson's beer makers were consistently popular, however, and eventually grew into substantial businesses.

Both the Peninsular Brewery and the Eberle Brewing Company grew from modest brewing shops to beermaking centers of factory dimensions. In the early 1900s, Caspar Haehnle II's Peninsular Brewery was making as many as 22,000 barrels of beer annually and Carl Eberle's brewery wasn't far behind. A 1912 promotional booklet for the city of Jackson boasted that Eberle's "bottled goods are shipped all over the state, many cities having large demands for the goods made by this model and clean brewery...Its customers, whether large or small, are always satisfied." This remained true even through the era of Prohibition.

The Jackson County government had adopted anti-alcohol laws by the 1920s while the federal government moved toward national prohibition laws. Jackson's Eberle Brewing became the Eberle Bottling Company during the Prohibition era and the firm began producing only soda pop. Other beer bottlers followed suit. With Prohibition's repeal in December of 1933, the Eberle Company, and others, returned to beer production. The increasing prominence of nationally-organized brewers and distributors, however, contributed to the demise of Jackson's beermakers. Eberle, the last of Jackson's local breweries, closed its doors in 1964.

A. Weber's "City Saloon" was located just down the street from Loeser's, at 220 East Main. The round, painted metal advertisements for the city's local brews are clearly visible on the tavern's doorposts. Saloons such as these provided a meeting space for the city's industrial workers and such public taverns and bars became increasingly popular with the growing number of leisure hours and increased pocket money afforded by work in the city's factories.

This saloon was one of many in Downtown Jackson on Michigan Avenue during the 1880s and 1890s. Note the sign painted on the building to the right which advertised 'Jaxon' brand soap, manufactured by the Central City Soap Company.

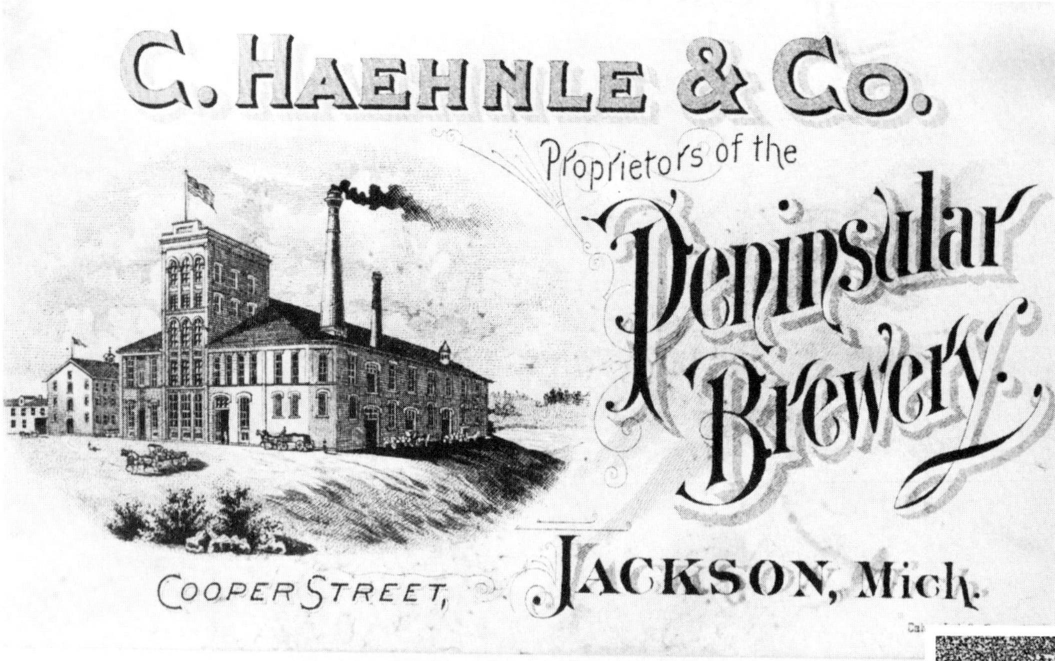

1870–1948

The Peninsular Brewery was opened by Caspar Haehnle II, a German immigrant who came to Jackson in 1867 to join his father and family. The large, brick-construction brewery was built in 1892, replacing an older wooden structure that had burned. Haehnle's son, Caspar III, took over the brewery's management in 1895, and the family ran the business until its close in 1948.

Caspar Haehnle

Workers at the Eberle Brewing Company posed before their bottling machine. Before the invention of the mechanical bottler like the one pictured in this photograph, workers bottled and capped the beer by hand before it was packaged into crates for distribution. Almost all of Jackson's saloons and bars featured Eberle's product.

Pictured above is an early photograph of the Eberle Brewing Company's crew. The man sitting second from left — with the dog between his legs — is Carl Eberle, Sr. Eberle Brewing employed its own cooper to make the kegs for the company's beer. Other tools of the trade can be seen in the photograph.

Before the widespread availability of cars or trucks, Eberle distributed beer to saloons throughout the city by horse-drawn wagon (below). Here, the brewery's teams are loaded up and posed before their brick facility, ca. 1908. Carl Eberle, Sr. can be seen standing on a delivery dock and his son, Carl Eberle, Jr., stands third from right, before the largest of the three teams.

The Loeser tavern, located at 210 East Main, was fairly typical of Jackson's saloons in the 1880s. During those peak years of the city's industrial development, Jackson was host to over seventy saloons. The majority of them were located on the east end of Main Street, near the city's industrial core. Note the advertisement for Haehnle's beer in the lower left and right hand corners.

"I'm drinking Eberles." This serving tray and others like it were probably a common sight in many of Jackson's early saloons. Eberle's produced over eight different kinds of beer, including traditional, seasonal brews with 'Blue Star Beer' as their most popular brand. With the onset of Prohibition in the late 1910s, Eberle began to phase out beer production and concentrated on its soft drink products instead. With the repeal of prohibition in 1933, Eberle again began brewing beer.

This bar, known as simply The Pub, was located on Greenwood Avenue for many years and is remembered as a popular local gathering place.

Ice & Refrigeration

Before the invention of electric refrigerators, cooling food and other perishable items remained the task of ice makers and ice box manufacturers. The earliest ice and refrigeration companies used natural refrigerants, harvesting ice from the frozen lakes of the northern U.S. during the late winter months. The snow was removed from the lake's surface by horse-drawn 'scrapers' and then scored and cut with an 'ice plow' to create even-sized blocks of ice. Groups of men worked with picks and poles to float the blocks to insulated storage houses built near the lake's edge. It was then packed in layers of sawdust for use in the hot summer months. Several early Jackson companies were involved in ice and refrigeration.

The Jackson Ice Company was formed in 1883 and serviced Jackson city residents until 1914. The frozen water was cut from Devil's Lake, in Lenawee County, and stored in a lakeside ice house and was shipped into the city by rail during the summer months for use in consumers' ice boxes. But ice delivery services weren't the only Jackson industries involved in ice and refrigeration.

The Metal Stamping Company was incorporated in 1904 and made round, metal ice boxes for almost ten years. The White Frost was unusual for its round form. Most ice boxes were more or less rectangular and, most often, made of wood. The Metal Stamping Company's oddly shaped products were painted a white enamel, had revolving shelves and were advertised as a "Safeguard of the family's health."

The Jackson Cold Storage Company's creators conceived of ice boxes on a different scale and built a plant in 1903 that was, essentially, an enormous ice box. The company was run by William Reynolds, E.W. Crafts and W.K. Sagendorph and their building contained 55,000 cubic feet of cooled storage space dispersed throughout four stories. The company used only natural ice and its rooms were cooled by an icy brine that was prepared in the top of the building and circulated through a complex system of piping. The company eventually disappeared after the introduction of cheap and efficient means of artificial refrigeration.

Ice and ice boxes were used in Jackson and other cities as late as the 1940s, when they gave way to the now-familiar electric refrigerators pioneered during the 1920s and '30s.

Delivery men for Jackson's Consumers Ice and Fuel Company brought the customers' ice by horse-drawn wagon. Tales are often told of ice men or milkmen who walked near their wagon: the horse did the driving, stopping at each house along the route. The horse often remembered the various places where deliveries were regularly made, and the only part of the job left to the delivery man was hefting the product into the customers' homes.

Pictured left is the Jackson Cold Storage Company's ice house and storage facility. The refrigeration company stored a thousand tons of ice every season for use throughout the summer. Built in 1903, the plant was filled with perishable items bought during market gluts. They were then sold off when the price had risen significantly enough to make a profit. As refrigeration technologies improved, the Jackson Cold Storage Company's facilities became obsolete. (Photo from *Held At Zero.)*

Jackson's Metal Stamping Company began producing the White Frost Sanitary Refrigerator and the Jack Frost refrigerator in 1904. The 'refrigerators' were really ice boxes, unique because of their round, metal design. A top-opening compartment stored the ice and some models came equipped with a side-mounted water cooler. (Advertisement from April 1915 issue of *The Modern Priscilla.)*

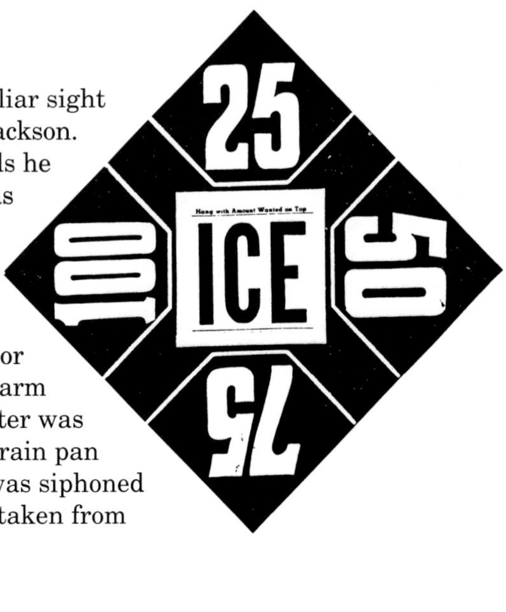

The ice man was a familiar sight in turn-of-the-century Jackson. When making his rounds he looked for a sign, such as the one pictured here, to let him know how many pounds of ice were needed. Large ice blocks would last a day or even a little longer in warm weather and melted water was either emptied from a drain pan beneath the ice box or was siphoned off to a drain. (Graphic taken from *American Ice Boxes.)*

Pictured above are Jackson Ice Company workers leading horse-drawn ice scrapers over Devil's Lake. These scrapers acted as gigantic scooping plows, removing the snow from the lake's frozen surface to make cutting easier and more accurate. The rig on the far left is an ice scorer: it was used to score lines into the ice as cutting guides.

Two ice cutters (right) pose near their gasoline-powered ice cutter. The 1920s rotary blade design was a far cry from the earlier, horse-drawn 'ice plows' used to cut block ice during the nineteenth century.

Here, Jackson Ice Company workers pose among the scaffolding and conveyors connected to the Devil's Lake ice house. This structure descended to meet the lake's edge. Workers pushed the 100 plus-pound blocks of ice up the enormous ramps to be slid down into the ice house. The ramps were raised as the ice and its insulation filled the storage structure.

The Hayes Wheel Company's 'Old Timer's Club,' in 1912. The club was a group of long-term Hayes employees who gathered together to enjoy Michigan's relaxing summer days.

From Autos to Auto Parts

During Jackson's automobile manufacturing days many local machine shops and foundries moved into a natural role: they became suppliers of parts and machinery for carmakers. Parts' suppliers had long been a part of Jackson's earlier carriage industry. Wheels, springs, upholstery and carriage tops were made by specialty companies like the Shepherd Brake Company and the Lewis Spring and Axle Company. One of Jackson's first parts' suppliers, the National Wheel Company, was formed in 1889 and made 200,000 wheels every year for local carriage makers. When the automobile began to supplant carriages and buggies as everyday transportation, most of the city's producers of carriage and wagon parts became, instead, manufacturers of auto parts.

When Jackson carmakers began to flourish in the early 1900s, so too did makers of automobile parts and accessories. Smaller manufacturers grew up around the car producers. Some made whole assemblies like wheels or engines while others cast or machined small, metal parts. Companies making finished automobiles slowly began to disappear in Jackson after 1918 and the city's automobile parts' makers were, in fact, destined to outlive the carmakers. The local manufacturing focus grew steadily into one of machining, forging and casting automotive parts and supplies.

Numerous companies formed in Jackson to support the city's expanding carriage and auto interests. One of these, the Shepherd Brake Company, was formed in 1894.

William C. Durant and J.D. Dort, of Flint's Durant-Dort Carriage Company, bought the Jackson Wheel Company in 1889 and formed the Imperial Wheel Company. The wheelmaker was located at Ganson and Wisner and it employed 350 men. Raw materials were shipped into Jackson by rail from Tennessee and Kentucky and the iron-banded, wooden wheels were used by the local carriage-making factories as well as by numerous factories in Flint. Imperial stopped producing wheels in 1905, when Durant moved production facilities for the Buick Motor Company into the plant.

Hayes Wheel

A Hayes Wheel Company delivery truck fully loaded with a shipment of wooden automobile wheels.

C. B. Hayes

In 1908, C.B. Hayes — former vice-president of the Imperial Wheel Company — formed the Hayes Wheel Company. Hayes eventually became one of the largest suppliers of wheels to not only Jackson's automakers, but to Detroit's car factories as well. In the picture above, a Hayes delivery truck is loaded with a shipment of wooden wheels for use on trucks and automobiles. Hayes Wheel Company bought what had been the Imperial Wheel Company's plant at Ganson and Wisner streets in 1921. The plant had housed many Jackson automotive concerns, including both the Buick and Marion-Handley carmakers. In 1927, Hayes merged with the Kelsey Wheel Company of Detroit, to form the Kelsey-Hayes Company.

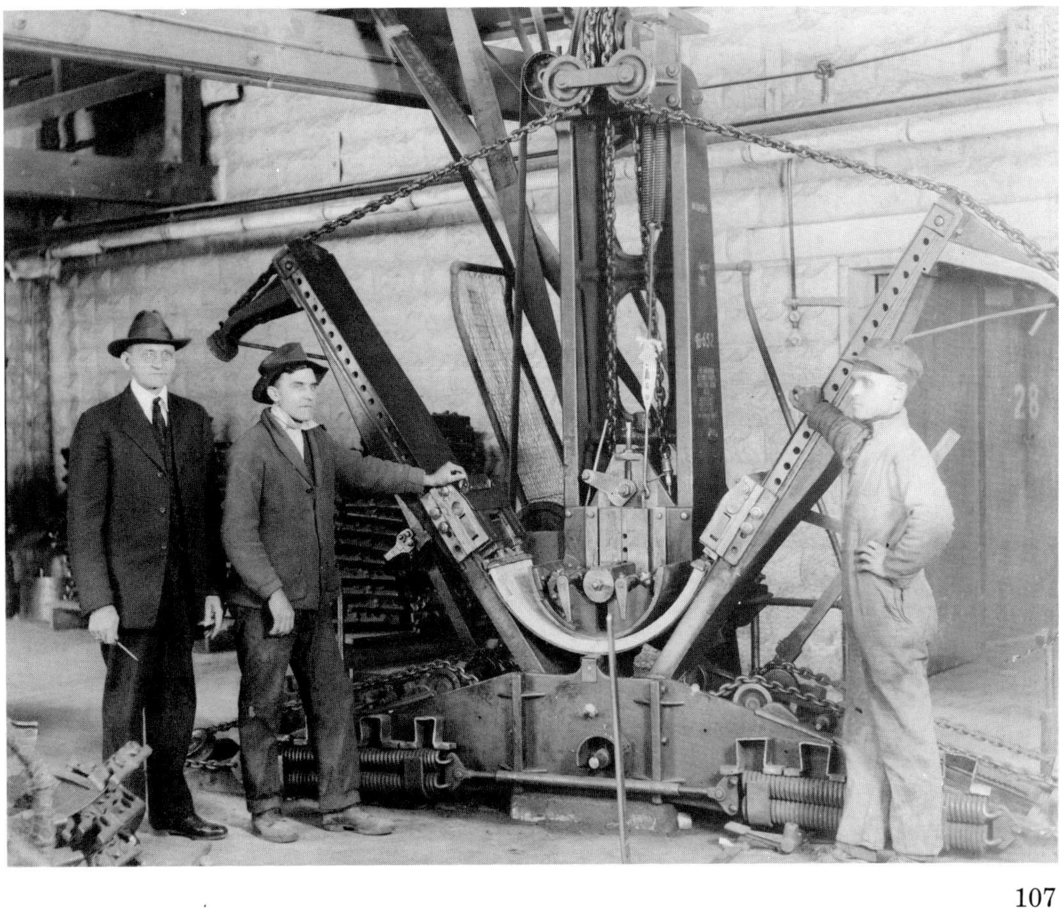

Presses such as the one pictured here, were used by the Hayes Wheel Company to make steel rims and other formed-steel components.

Kent-Moore

Numerous smaller companies formed in Jackson to produce auto parts or related accessories. One of these, the Electric Intake Heater Company, began producing small electric accessories for various popular auto models in 1918. Another, the Kent-Moore Organization produced specialty tools for the repair and maintenance of various car models. Kent-Moore was established by John Moore and William Kent, who bought another small Jackson auto accessories firm named Hinckley-Myers.

William Kent

John Moore

Jackson's small parts shops often grew into larger plants. The Frost Gear and Forge Company began business in 1907 when E.J. and C.M. Frost formed a partnership. The gear maker's original shop was a small, one story building and they employed about thirty-five men. Shortly after its incorporation, however, the company outgrew its facilties and bought the former site of a Jackson flouring equipment maker. By 1929, Frost employed nearly 500 men and women. This aerial view shows Frost as it appeared in the late 1920s, shortly before the Clark Equipment Company purchased the factory in 1930.

Thorrez-Maes

The Thorrez-Maes Manufacturing Company was started by Camiel and Henry Thorrez and Victor Maes, three Belgian immigrants who had decided to make Jackson their home in the early 1900s. Camiel Thorrez moved to Jackson in 1912 and helped to start the Jackson Screw Machine Company, which he soon left behind to help organize Thorrez-Maes in 1926. The company produced a wide variety of small, machined products that were mainly used by the auto industry: gear blanks, bolts, nuts, brake pins and other products were made from bars of steel. The company employed over 250 workers just before the Second World War and the company's payroll increased when Thorrez-Maes became involved in war production, making bullets, aircraft engine parts and other wartime products. In 1948, a series of union disputes led Thorrez to announce that the company's assets would be liquidated and the plant sold. A new screw-machine products company, C. Thorrez Industries was started by Thorrez and continues to be run by the family.

The E.C. Clark Motor Company supplied finished engines for use in the Jackson Automobile Corporation's first cars. Here, mechanics assemble and adjust eight cylinder engines, ca. 1915.

Hancock Industries was located at 225 North Horton Street. The company produced an entire line of metal parts and automobile accessories such as door locks, hood locks, deck locks and hood hinges.

Lockwood Ash

Fred T. and A.L. Lockwood opened an "Automobile Storage and Repairing" business in 1903, occupying the site formerly held by Jackson automobile pioneer B.J. Carter. The Lockwood brothers produced several experimental cars around 1906, but they never went into any consistent production. Fred Lockwood eventually became one of the founding interests in the Lockwood-Ash Motor Company, located at East Main and Horton. In addition to car parts the Lockwood-Ash Company became a substantial producer of outboard marine engines and the company was eventually purchased by Johnson Motors of Milwaukee, Wisconsin.

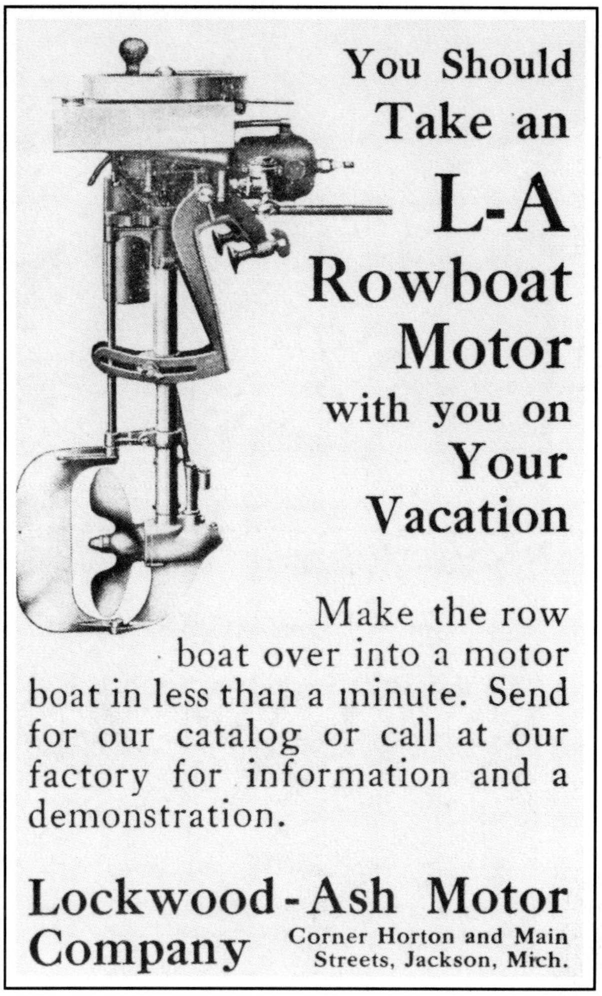

Lockwood Ash advertisement for their boat motors.

The surge in demand for automobile parts during the 1920s spurred on the development of companies like the Chromium Plating Corporation, pictured above, and the Jackson Motor Shaft Company, shown below. Both companies continued to do a thriving business long after the last finished automobile rolled off of a Jackson automaker's assembly line.

Gas Stations

In addition to auto parts' makers, the success of the automobile in Jackson helped give rise to other businesses. Gas stations and automobile service centers — which we often take for granted today — began to appear on street corners all over the city. Names that are familiar today began to appear on gasoline franchises throughout Jackson: Standard, Gulf, Sunoco or Texaco.

Standard Oil was one of the first major gasoline companies in Jackson and, at one time, had over eleven service stations throughout the city. The gasoline service station even made its appearance outside of the city limits and often began to assume the role of a small general store as well.

The Watts-Morehouse Company, located at the far eastern end of Michigan Avenue, was a producer of automobile trunks.

Among the many small companies that began during the war years was Dawlen Corporation. In 1942, Ed Small began a screw machine products' business in this modest building. Dawlen Corporation has since grown into one of Jackson's most successful machining industries. They continue to produce automotive parts.

Employees of Jackson Steel Products Company posed for this photograph outside of their factory, ca. 1918. The company was a subsidiary of General Motors, producing automobile wheels.

From the beginnings of the auto industry, and even more so today, many car accessories weren't produced by the car's maker, but were produced by smaller, outside contract corporations instead. Jackson's Ryerson and Haynes, Inc., was one of these. From its beginning in 1927, Ryerson and Haynes was connected to the auto industry but the company gave car producers an extra lift in 1934 when Steven DeOrlow, a Ryerson and Haynes employee, invented the bumper jack. The company did a steady business throughout the years producing bumper jacks, chiefly for Chevrolet. Jacks weren't the only accessory that the company produced, however: car grills, metal tire covers and other parts were also produced by Ryerson and Haynes. The company left its Ganson Street location, pictured here ca. 1930, in 1969 for a modernized facility in the Micor Industrial Park.

Sparks-Withington

One of Jackson's most prominent makers of car parts went into business long before the city had become a 'car parts town.' In 1900 Philip and Winthrop Withington, sons of prominent Jacksonian, William Withington, formed a company to make metal parts of all sorts. Their primary customer was their father: they made metal components for the Withington-Cooley farm tools company. But shortly after the company's founding, the Withington brothers hired William Sparks, a local Jackson man who had emigrated to America from England at the age of fourteen. Sparks began his career at the newly-formed company as a bookkeeper. Before being hired by the Withingtons, he worked for a local grocer and was a press operator in a Jackson factory, as well. Sparks brought a knowledge of pressed metal production and a sharpened sales ability to the new company.

William Sparks introduced the idea of changing the way the Withingtons made their products, from more traditional wrapping and welding techniques to the use of large metal presses. The idea was successful. The Withington brothers made William Sparks the general manager of their plant and the firm's name was changed to the Sparks-Withington Company. Although the company had started making farm tool components and carriage parts, its equipment was easily converted and it soon switched to automobile parts as Jackson and Detroit car makers began to prosper.

In 1913, company leaders decided to go into the manufacture of warning signals for automobiles: they would make car horns. A trade name for the new product was needed, and the first four letters of the name 'Sparks' and the last three letters of the name 'Withington' were combined to form Sparton. Sparton horns were first used by the Hudson Motor Car Company and many other famous car companies followed Hudson's lead. The Sparton horn became very successful, often with great help from William Sparks' aggressive sales techniques.

When the United States entered the first World War, Sparks-Withington devoted itself to war production, making everything from hand-operated gas warning signals to hand grenades to steel helmets. Sparton also produced radiators that were used by the Packard Motor Company for use on its Liberty aircraft engine. After the close of the war, the company resumed production of Sparton horns and began developing new products as well. The most important of these was the radio.

The Sparks-Withington Company founders: Winthrop Withington, Phillip Withington and William Sparks.

In 1926, when Sparks-Withington produced its first experimental sets, radios were powered by batteries only. Vacuum tubes that could be mass-produced had not yet been developed, and the company set up a laboratory in Cleveland for research and development. Headed by Charles J. Kayko, the Cleveland lab worked to develop a working and inexpensive way to make vacuum tubes. By 1928, Sparton radios containing Kayko's tube were being mass manufactured by Sparks-Withington.

Toward the end of the 1930s, Sparks-Withington began research on television production and several experimental models were produced between 1939 and 1941, when the United States entered the second World War. The company produced many sophisticated products for the war effort, among them a training device for airplane turret gunners. The company also made bomb release controls, parts for the Thompson machine gun and airplane radio equipment. Following the close of the war, Sparks-Withington returned to production of automobile horns, radios and television sets.

Pictured at left is William Sparks.

An aerial view of the Sparks-Withington Company's main production facility, ca. 1935. Note the walls of the old prison to the right of the factory. The factory was located on the site of the old Withington-Cooley Company, which had made extensive use of contracted convict labor.

Cross Country Trip

In the summer of 1915, William Sparks requested that his two sons, Harry and Cliff, make a trip to the west coast along the newly constructed Lincoln and National Highways. Sparks wanted his sons to erect signs along the highways which proclaimed 'Safety First, Sound Sparton.' The signs were to be put up near dangerous curves, hills, blind spots and other points of danger as both a service and an advertisement.

The two young men embarked on their 'summer job' in a Model 'T' Ford truck that had been especially painted with the Sparton logo and various slogans, including the now famous 'The World Takes What Jackson Makes.' In one letter home from Los Angeles, late in August, Harry Sparks cabled his father with the message "Numerous detours it is impossible to erect many signs. Had to push car most of way over San Luis mountains. Top brake lining burned out so took off crank case and replaced it, and found broken pin; had one forged. Had car towed up two hills by mule team and started on the way."

Despite such difficulties, Clifford and Harry Sparks made their trip safely and successfully, erecting hundreds of Sparton signs.

Clifford (left) and Harry Sparks stand beside the 'Safety First, Sound Sparton' truck which they took across the country in 1915.

Harry and Cliff Sparks pound in their last sign on the Lincoln Highway, Golden Gate Park, San Francisco, after over thirty days on the road.

Jackson's Cascades

One of Jackson's best-known landmarks was built under the direction of William Sparks. The Cascades were commissioned by the William and Matilda Sparks Foundation in the fall of 1929. The Sparks envisioned an illuminated set of waterfalls and fountains that would form the centerpiece of a green and wooded `meditation center' for Jackson's citizens.

Work on the Cascades began in the spring of 1931. Eighty men were employed and worked by hand to produce the 550-foot long structure of reinforced concrete. The timing of the Cascades' construction was especially fortuitous and brought much-needed employment to Jackson's workers.

The Cascades have been one of Jackson's summertime traditions ever since its construction over fifty years ago.

Jackson's Gas Light Era

Before the advent of electricity and electric lighting, gas was used as the most common source of urban illumination. Streetlights — in cities that were wealthy enough to afford them — were first powered by coal gas that was piped into the lamp jets. The first such use of gas for urban lighting came in 1804 when Frederick Albert Winsor began promoting its use in London. The idea traveled across the Atlantic, and in the U.S., Baltimore was the first city to install a gas streetlight system. The city council passed an ordinance in late June of 1816 that authorized the Gas Light Company of Baltimore to install a lighting system. Gas lighting was slow in catching on, though, and almost forty years after the Baltimore company had installed its successful lighting system, only thirty urban communities in the U.S. were home to gas production plants and streetlights.

In 1857, Jackson joined a growing number of gas-lit cities when the Jackson Gas Light Company was organized. Several prominent citizens, among them Peter B. Loomis and S.W. Whitwell, helped to finance the company, which built gas-production 'works' on Clinton Street. The new gas service was a success and by 1881 the company had installed thirteen and one half miles of street mains and they serviced almost 120 street lamps. The Jackson Gas Light Company didn't use locally-mined coal in its gas-making process: coal was brought in from Pittsburgh over Jackson's railroad connections, because of the higher quality of coal available from out of state. By the 1880s, the gas company served over 500 local customers, who bought their fuel by the cubic foot. Jackson's going rate for gas was about two dollars and fifty cents per thousand cubic feet for heavy customers, and three dollars for lighter users.

As more and more cities became interested in gas illumination for their streets, new methods for producing gas were invented and old methods were made more efficient. Jackson became home to a second gas supplier in 1888. The Jackson National Gas Light and Fuel Company began its water-based gas production at the corner of Milwaukee and Franklin streets in 1887. The company's Chicago directors felt that Jackson, with its heavy industry and growing population, was a good place to begin their gas utility service. Unlike Jackson's first gas supplier, National Gas Light and Fuel pushed the use of its product for cooking, heating and for use by industry in gas-burning steam engines. Its gas was different from the typical coal-based type: the gas was produced by a chemical reaction using carbide-based chemicals and water. The carbide process made it easier to produce much larger volumes of gas at cheaper prices. National Gas Light and Fuel sold its gas at the meager price of thirty cents per thousand cubic feet.

The various gas makers and their installation of services in Jackson brought streetlighting and private use of gas into the city. The use of gas also brought new skills and sales opportunities for local merchants and blacksmiths. Pipefitters were needed to install and repair the elaborate systems of piping, both underground and within buildings. Meter installers and readers made their rounds and Jackson's dry goods stores began handling stoves, heaters and small appliances that used gas as a fuel.

A view of the Jackson Gas Company's offices and showrooms, ca. 1912. The showrooms were located on South Mechanic Street and all sorts of gas-powered lighting equipment and appliances were sold there.

The gaslight era faded from most urban areas in the United States during the 1880s, but lived on, for many years, in rural America. Remote farms — far from the short transmission lines of the early electric companies — often installed 'personal' gas systems to light and heat their homes. Carbide gas machines were popular with American farmers and other rural dwellers. The Night Commander Lighting Company was a small Jackson firm that produced a machine called the 'Night Commander Generator.'

Night Commander's product was a contraption (resembling a water heater) that was almost completely buried under ground (see photo right). It consisted of a cylindrical water tank into which small carbide pellets would drop, producing an inflammable gas that would fill the tank, for heating and lighting purposes.

The generator was ideal for small farms and rural dwellings because it worked with an automatic regulator to produce as much gas as needed in areas where gas and electrical services were practically unknown. It wouldn't be until the 1930s, when Consumers Power pushed ahead with its rural electrification project, that gas-makers like the Night Commander went out of style.

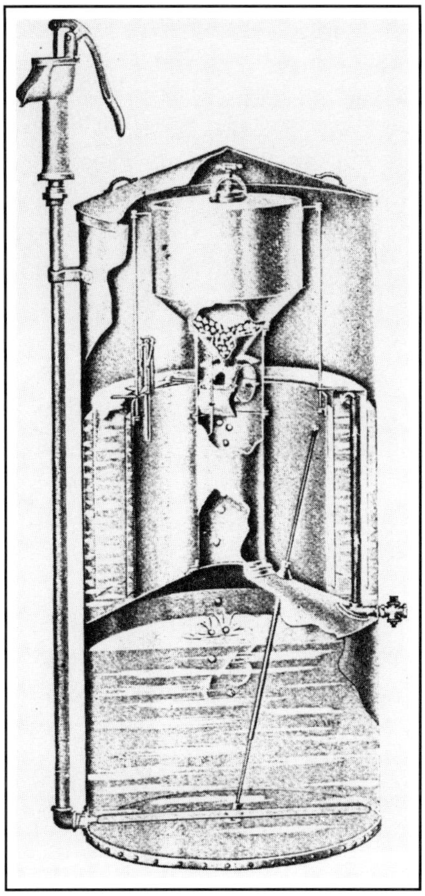

A wagon emblazoned with Night Commander promotionals participated in a Jackson parade, ca. 1915. Note the 'Jackson Cartage Company' sign on the wagon's bed.

Consumers Power

In the earliest days of electricity and electric lighting, there were no large power companies: most users of electricity owned a small generator of their own and would make power for their particular needs. It wasn't long, though, before the first power companies were created to distribute electricity for profit. In the late winter of 1888, William A. Foote and Samuel Jarvis incorporated one such company, naming it the Jackson Electric Light Works. Foote and Jarvis had supplied electric lighting to Jackson's downtown area as early as 1886, but by 1888 they were looking to expand their services to private homes and businesses.

William A. Foote

Foote acted as a tireless promoter for the new company, acquiring city service franchises and water rights througout central Michigan, from Jackson to Kalamazoo. Along with his brother, James and his partner, Samuel Jarvis, Foote set about building what would someday become Michigan's largest utility. A formative event in the utility company's history came on September 20, 1899, when the first long-distance high-voltage transmission was made over twenty-four miles of iron wire, between the Trowbridge Dam on the Kalamazoo River and the city of Kalamazoo. This unprecendented long-distance transmission of high-voltage power was made possible by the invention of an oil circuit, or "wagon box" switch by James B. Foote and George Stecker. The development of this switch along with other similar innovations allowed the Foote brothers and Jarvis to begin uniting remote hyrdraulic and steam generation sites throughout Michigan with populated areas needing power. Their dreams of an integrated network of electrical power was on its way to being realized.

The electric streetcar and interurban, electric lights and a proliferation of electrical appliances pushed the demand for electricity and William Foote kept expanding. In 1904, Foote began consolidating his various holdings into a larger corporation, to be called Commonwealth Power Company. Six years later, Commonwealth joined with other Michigan power suppliers to form Consumers Power Company, incorporated as a holding company under the laws of Maine. By the dawning of the 1930s, Consumers had become one of the largest utilities in the nation: a prominence that was reflected in its new headquarters, built in 1927 in downtown Jackson.

Consumers Power's growth during its first few decades of operations was phenomenal: in 1921 the company had 130,000 electrical customers and by 1940, that number had grown to almost 470,000. The utility continually added new facilities and new areas of service during the 1930s. One Consumers campaign aimed at bringing electrical service to rural areas. At the time, most work on the farm was still powered by muscle—both human and animal. Electrically powered machines for farming didn't really exist yet. But as Consumers Power and other similar utilities pushed their services further into rural areas, use of electrically powered equipment became more prevalent. When Consumers began its farm-electrification campaign in 1924, only three percent of Michigan's farmers were wired for power. By 1949, the utility was serving 100,000 farmers.

Following the passage of the Public Utilities Act of 1935, the Commonwealth and Southern Corporation — Consumers Power's parent holding company — began to be dismantled. The enormous company's operations covered power service from as far north as northern Michigan to parts of Florida. The process of breaking the company into smaller operations was a long and difficult one, much opposed by Commonwealth and Southern's corporate leadership. By July 15, 1949, however, plans for the dismantling of the company were ratified and Jackson's Consumers Power Company was on its way toward independent operations.

Since that time, Consumers Power Company has expanded its power services in many areas, including the use of natural gas, pumped storage hydroelectric generation and nuclear power. It continues to supply energy to most of the lower peninsula of Michigan to this day.

This photo shows the original location of the Jackson Electric Light Works—Jackson's first utility, incorporated in 1888.

Trowbridge Dam as it appeared in 1899. It was here that the Foote brothers and their team of engineers proved the possibility of transmitting electricity over long distances. Experiments at the Trowbridge Dam paved the way for the much larger hydro-electric generation sites that were used extensively by Consumers Power.

James B. Foote, William Foote's younger brother, provided much of the technical genius behind the Trowbridge Dam project and was reputed to have been a 'born engineer.'

W.A. Foote's Commonwealth Power building, ca. 1910. The early utility's headquarters were located at the corner of Hayes and Michigan.

These Consumers Power Company towers held adjustable gas storage tanks. As gas consumption levels rose and fell, so too did the tanks within these gigantic steel frames. Note the long line of trucks near the base of the building. These were the Consumers Power Company's brand new line of Chevrolet service vehicle.

Installation crews, such as the group of men pictured below, worked to install the poles and wiring that brought power from Consumers' generators to consumers' homes.

Streetcars and Interurbans

Jackson received its first taste of electric streetcar service in September of 1891. It was an exciting day: on its inaugural run, the city's first streetcar encountered a problem with its 'trolley' connection to the live electrical wires that supplied its power. The trolley slipped from its overhead wire and, snapping up on its spring, severed a telephone line. The severed line fell onto the trolley line, causing a fire in a nearby wooden telephone box. When the horse-drawn fire truck arrived, the live line fell onto one of the horses, killing it instantly and causing general consternation. Despite the horrifying events of the streetcar's big day in Jackson, the city soon was being serviced by a network of electrically-powered rail cars.

Around the turn of the century, the same idea was applied to transportation between cities, as well. 'Interurbans,' as they became known, grew to be some of the early electric companies' biggest customers. In Jackson, William A. Foote became involved in the streetcar and electric railway business when he gained control of Jackson's trolley services. He began thinking of building an interurban line between Jackson and Ann Arbor sometime in 1900. A Detroit-based interurban company, the Detroit United System, began to develop a similar line at about the same time, but working from Ann Arbor to Jackson. While Foote was building his line east, J.D. Hawks and S.F. Angus were supervising a building project heading west. A race was on!

By the autumn of 1901, the Angus-Hawks project was well ahead of Foote's line. Foote was still over twenty miles out of Ann Arbor, while the Detroit United System men were reaching the outskirts of Jackson. Foote lost the race into Ann Arbor: the Angus-Hawks line reached Jackson well before Foote had even come close to Ann Arbor — but at a price. The Detroit men had concentrated on speeding up their construction, letting the quality of their rails and grades go down. They won the race, but their line was reputed to have a bumpy ride. Foote stopped his line at Grass Lake.

The venture wasn't a loss for Foote and his electric company, however. The practical experience in the construction of electrical railways gave Foote the knowledge he needed to expand his services elsewhere. Foote eventually built an enormously successful interurban line between Jackson and Battle Creek.

One of the many interurban lines servicing the Jackson area.

A view of the Consumers Power Club House at Clark Lake, ca. 1926. The club house was built by the men's Good Fellowship Club and the women's Commonwealth Club—both employee organizations.

Consumers Power linemen installing electrical power at the Jackson County Fairgrounds, ca. 1926

A view of the Consumers Power Company headquarters building, designed by Albert Kahn and built in 1927.

An Industrial City

Though the majority of Jackson's industrial interests centered around the automobile and the train, many other types of industries flourished in the city as well. A diverse array of products were manufactured in Jackson—from construction equipment and machines to refrigeration equipment and furniture.

The Jackson Fence Company made electrified 'Dog Shock' brand fence and other types of fence. The building on Francis near High Street was later used by the Fox Engineering Company.

The Michigan Seating Company, founded in 1907, was one of the last establishments in Jackson to utilize convict labor. The company's contract for two hundred prisoners expired in 1916, but they continued to produce wicker furniture for many years. The building on Wildwood still has the company name on the front.

This photo, ca. 1930, shows the original Dawn Food Products building at 330 Otsego. Dawn helped bring baking and food into Jackson's family of twentieth century industries. The Dawn Bakery was started at 112 East Michigan and by 1920 its products had become so popular, that a company was formed to sell patented baking mixes. The firm moved to the 330 Otsego location in 1920, and the bakery was closed as the company concentrated exclusively on making bakery mixes. After some belt-tightening during the Depression years, Dawn continued to expand to include not only 150 types of baking mix, but industrial food manufacturing equipment as well.

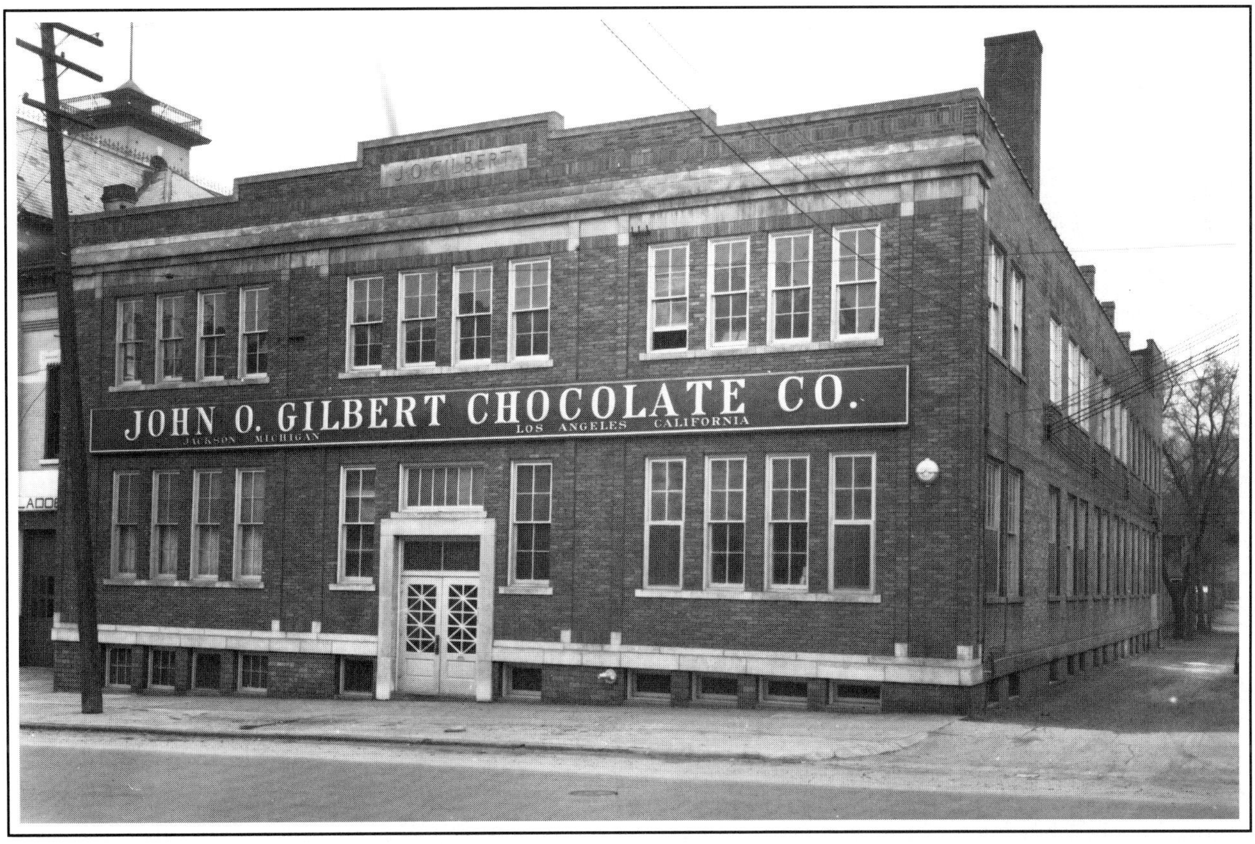

A view of the John Gilbert Candy Company as it appeared ca. 1935. Though the A.E. Brooks candymakers employed almost 200 people and Gilbert employed 35, Gilbert was the larger of the two confectioners. The company made use of mechanized production techniques and produced candies using industrial methods. The Gilbert Company's main factory (above) was located on Cortland Street, but it also kept a distribution store on Main that included a lunch and breakfast diner.

W.P. Emmons began an excavating company in the early years of the century. Using equipment such as pictured here, he dug basements for Jackson High School, East and West Intermediate Schools, and many downtown buildings.

In 1918, Emmons expanded his business by bidding on the garbage hauling contract with the city and winning! The company was originally located where Kuhl's Bell Tower Market now stands.

Some of Jackson's oldest companies survived well into the twentieth century, modifying their product lines as times changed. The Knickerbocker Company was one such company. Though originally a flouring-machine manufacturer, Knickerbocker later produced concrete mixing machinery, such as this 1920s 'Knickerbocker 10-S.' The company continued to change with the growth of new markets, making everything from woodworking machinery to fork trucks and fork truck attachments.

In 1907, C.H. Willbee formed the Willbee Concrete Products Company. Willbee grew to become one of Jackson's longest-lasting family-owned companies with four generations of family owners and leadership.

Jacksonian F.P. Miller began working in Jackson as a machinist for the Jackson Automobile Company. He eventually moved into car sales and repairs and in 1922 opened a business in car repair in the garage connected to his home at 607 N. Blackstone. Within several years he expanded his home business into a small machine shop and the business mushroomed. Miller had completely moved into larger facilities by 1937, and the company which he started in his modest garage at 607 N. Blackstone became one of Jackson's largest machining industries.

F.P. Miller

This picture shows F.P. Miller's garage at 607 N. Blackstone Street, where Miller Industries was born.

The Macklin Grinding Wheel Corporation turned out one of Jackson's more unusual products...industrial-size grinding wheels.

The Acme Corporation — manufacturers of refrigeration and cooling equipment —formed in 1919 and located within the city in 1932 when a fire destroyed their former plant. The company was originally a pipe distributor, but moved into the manufacturing of refrigeration units in the 1930s. Acme bought the former Withington-Cooley (American Fork and Hoe) buildings in the middle 1950s, and used them as warehousing and office buildings.

Jackson In The World Wars

At the outbreak of the Second World War, the Sparks-Withington Company was just getting into full production of its automobile horns. The company went into heavy war production both for the U.S. and Britain, and they made a diverse group of products: hand-operated gas warning signals for use in trenches, horns for combat vehicles, hand grenade assemblies, helmets and 75 mm shells.

Industrial corporations in Jackson, like their counterparts throughout the United States, made significant contributions to U.S. military efforts in both World Wars. Many of the city's largest companies, including Hayes Wheel, Briscoe Motors and Sparks-Withington, produced munitions, helmets, equipment and other supplies for the United States' First World War effort. In late 1917, several of Jackson's largest industrial producers joined together to form the Jackson Munitions Company, and contracts were signed for the production of 1,000,000 75-mm shells and almost 200,000 155-mm shells. At one point in 1918, the Briscoe Motors Corporation reached a daily production of 11,000 rifle grenades, manufacturing a total of 500,000 before the signing of the armistice. Though Jackson's World War One manufacturing effort was enormous, it paled in comparison with the dizzying output of Jackson companies during the Second World War.

By the time the United States entered into the Second World War, industrial manufacturers throughout the United States had already begun preparing for what seemed to be the inevitable entry of the U.S. into the war. "Europe is at war. It will be a world war," were the words of Sparks-Withington's company leaders. "We will eventually be drawn in, like it or not, either by the warring factions in Europe or more likely by direct conflict with Japan. Get your departments organized to handle the eventual increased volume which goes with war." The sentiments of Sparks-Withington's leaders were echoed by similar companies throughout the nation and, eventually, such predictions were borne out as the truth. In Jackson, hurried preparations were made and war production began almost immediately at almost all of the city's large industrial manufacturing sites. Munitions, electronic equipment, aviation supplies, training equipment (among many other products) were turned out in unprecedented quantities.

The swelling proportions of Jackson's wartime production brought about many drastic changes in the city's workplaces. One of the most striking was the increased prominence of women within the industrial workplace. Jackson women took on jobs that, previous to the war, had been held only by men. The women worked in line production, machine tools work, assembly, testing and shipping. By 1943, women made up almost 60% of Jackson's industrial workforce, a change that carried over beyond the war years to permanently change the character of the workforce in Jackson, and nationwide.

Sparks-Withington's largest contribution to the United States First World War effort was in making steel helmet frames for ground troops. Almost one-third of the steel helmets used by United States soldiers were made, in part, by Sparks-Withington.

Sparks-Withington

By the time the United States entered the Second World War, the Sparks-Withington Company had become a leading manufacturer of radios and had begun work on experimental television sets. Sparks-Withington had several British war contracts in 1939 and the company's leaders had prepared the Sparton factories and facilities for what seemed to be the United States' inevitable entry into the war. During the war years, the company produced a diverse run of products—from electric bomb releases to mobile transmitter vehicles.

The sensitive parts of electronic technologies like the Sparton radio compass or the Sparton radio equipment used by ground troops required thorough testing under extreme conditions. Here, female workers test parts for Sparton's radio compass.

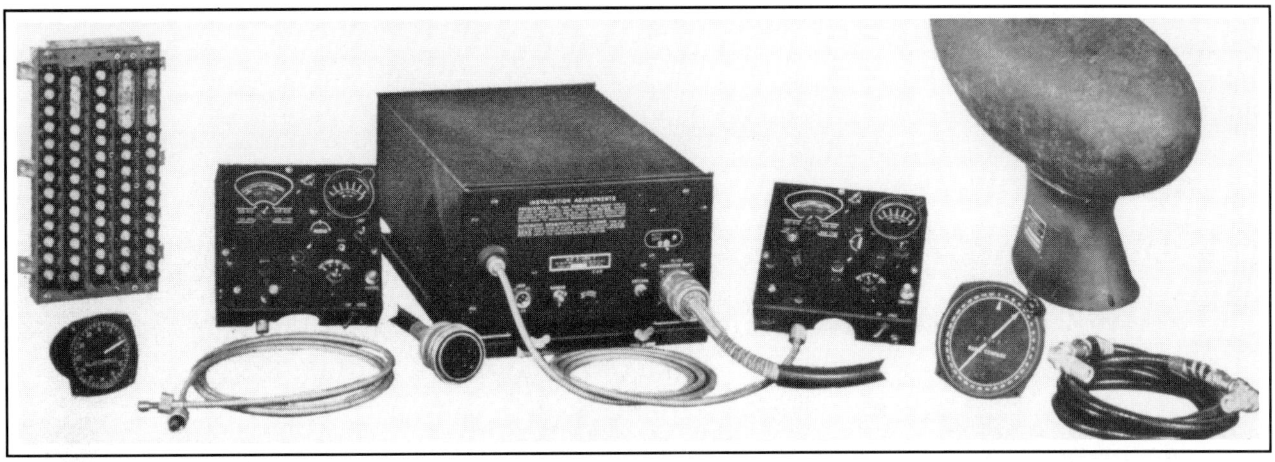

One of the most important of Sparton's World War II contributions was an airborne radio compass. The electronic compass allowed pilots to home in on radio beacons and to maintain steady flight paths.

Workers install wiring on Sparton C-3 flight Trainers, ca 1941. The small, wooden cockpit replicas were used by the U.S. armed forces to train pilots. The instruments inside the trainer were simulated aircraft instuments and a series of motors and tracking devices simulated the motions of flight while recording the student pilot's performance on a piece of paper for later review.

A worker at the Handley-Brown Heater Company performs a welding operation on a 90-mm gun component.

The Jackson branch of the Clark Equipment Company produced lift trucks, such as these, by the thousands. Industrial lifts, movers and fork-trucks improved the efficiency of both the army and civilian companies.

German native Peter J. Hurst came to the United States shortly before the outbreak of World War II. He had come to the U.S. in 1939 on an international business trip, looking to gain contracts for Rotadisk, a German corporation. One week after his arrival in New York, Hitler ordered the blitz on Poland, and World War II had erupted. Hurst proceeded to visit American airplane parts manufacturers, searching for an existing corporation to manufacture his reusable hydraulic-hose fittings under licensing agreement. It was at this time that he met Charles Hollerith, Vice President of Jackson's Hayes Industries, through the Navy Bureau of Aeronautics.

Peter Hurst inspects employee operations in Jackson's Aeroquip plant, ca. 1945. Aeroquip's main product was a reusable flexible hose fitting that could be taken off or attached quickly and easily, a valuable product during wartime emergency repairs.

Hurst's meeting with Hollerith and with other prominent Jackson businessmen resulted in the formation of the Aeroquip Corporation. On April 26, 1940, Aeroquip was officially incorporated with ten investors contributing $1,000 each. With the increasingly enormous importance of airplanes and aerospace to the war effort, Hurst found a ready market for his product—reusable hose fittings for aeronautic hydraulic systems. Almost one year after its founding, the new company had 100 employees, all under Hurst's direction. But because of his status as a German immigrant, Hurst was excluded from Aeroquip's production facilities for almost 21 months. With the U.S. entry into the war, Hurst was classified as an enemy alien and ordered away from Aeroquip's production areas. Hurst was eventually brought in to help smooth production difficulties.

General Products' president, Russell Bengel, presided over the company's acceptance of an 'E' award on August 6, 1945. The Army-Navy 'E' award was given to companies recognized for outstanding service in war production. Many Jackson businesses received the award.

Three General Products' employees posed for this photograph after returning home from the war. From left to right: Joe Moll, Herbert Boyels, Frank Safidlo.

In June of 1941, General Products received initial orders to build assembly parts for Aerial Demolition bombs and by December 4th, 1941, 67% of the entire plant facilities was dedicated to the war effort. By August of 1942, the plant capacity had increased by approximately 45% and the entire plant facilities were devoted to war work. Around the clock workers produced small steel castings for a variety of war products, including 3-inch shells, rockets, bombs and combat vehicles.

"Prosperous Times: Jackson After World War II"

The character of much of Jackson's industrial life changed drastically after the close of the Second World War. A feeling of national prosperity that had been dimmed or lost during the Depression years returned when most of the nation's enormous industrial capacity was turned over to peacetime production. In Jackson, companies that had been intensively involved in war work found themselves in a position to re-focus on the production of consumer goods. Companies like Western Stamping, Aeroquip and the Sparks-Withington Company converted to peacetime consumer markets. Many other changes helped to contribute to Jackson's general prosperity in the post-war years.

The surge in nationwide demand for large consumer products, particularly the automobile, had strong effects on Jackson. Local machine shops, foundries and automobile parts' producers experienced an unprecedented period of growth. Other changes were just as influential: altered views of women's roles in the home and at work, a national population surge — later known as the 'Baby Boom' — and the invention and development of new consumer products, such as solid state radios or television sets, had local influences on Jackson's economic growth.

In the photo at left, Western Stamping Company employee, Elizabeth Krutsch, sorts parts for a toy cash register. Western Stamping, which had got its start in 1939, was a small 'job stamping' firm. The company did mainly war contract work until the war's end and in 1946 the directors were seeking to liquidate the company. In 1946, a local man named Lathrup Barry approached Western Stamping with a toy cash register and the company's directors decided to attempt going into production. By the end of 1946, Western Stamping's first toy was on department store shelves. The company soon expanded its line to include toy banks, toy cash registers and many others. Like many manufacturing firms in the post-war years, the majority of Western Stamping's employees were women working in light assembly positions.

Aeroquip

Following the close of the Second World War, the demands for Aeroquip's products which had been created by U.S. and Allied military needs fell off dramatically. The company's leaders began to investigate new markets, particularly in commercial aerospace and in the growing needs of the industrial hydraulics field. The company's founder, Peter Hurst, pursued Aeroquip's growth with the same vigor he had given to its war work and by the first years of the 1950s, Aeroquip was in a state of consistent expansion. Aeroquip relied heavily on small parts' producers in the Jackson area.

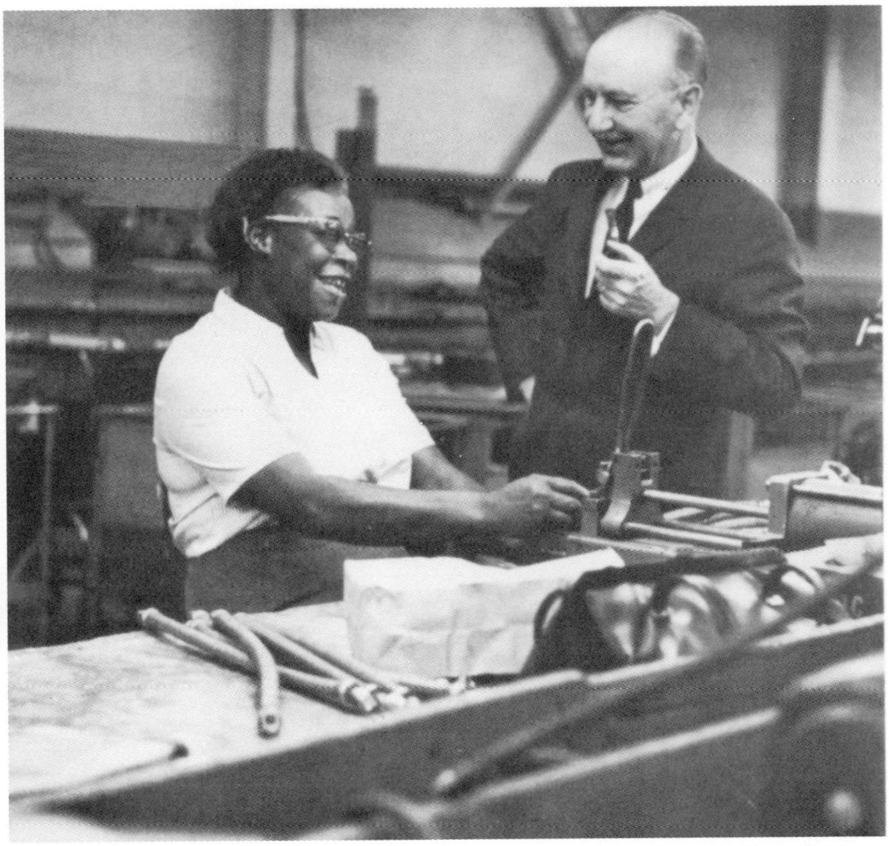

Aeroquip founder, Peter Hurst, remained in close contact with his employees throughout his years as the company's director.

The number of women employed by Aeroquip increased during the war years — a situation which carried over long after 1945. The woman pictured at left, Myrtle Foster, began working for the company in 1942 and worked the Jackson plant for over thirty-five years.

Fox Engineering

The Fox Engineering Company became a part of Jackson's industrial community in 1916 when Kathleen and Hiram Fox moved from Grand Rapids into a small building on Ganson Street. In 1938, the company moved into the former site of the Jackson Fence Company, on Francis Street (right). Fox made custom design machinery for a wide variety of industrial customers, including all of the large automakers. Following the close of the Second World War, Robert M. German took the position of general manager and was named president of the company within eight years. The business was one of Jackson's last thriving custom machine tools makers, and it benefitted enormously from the prosperous times following the close of the war. The company designed and built almost four thousand pieces of custom machinery and only recently closed its doors.

This enormous machine pictured below, built by Fox Engineering for General Motors, weighed 48,000 pounds and was equipped with ten electrical motors with a combined horsepower of 43 1/2. Such behemoth machines were common Fox products.

Clark Equipment

The Clark Equipment Company entered Jackson's industrial life in 1928 when the company's directors acquired the Frost Gear and Forge Company. Clark immediately began developing its Jackson facility as a part of the company's transmission assembly operations. Following the war, however, Clark's business volume increased almost ten times. With the boom in postwar industrial production, Clark's principal products,—forklifts and other industrial 'movers'—were in high demand. The company's Jackson branch prospered and all of Clark's truck transmission assembly and production operations were moved into their Jackson plant. Clark remained one of Jackson's major employers throughout the city's post-war economic boom.

Many social events were organized for Clark employees. Clark workers and their families plyed, watched and cheered for the company's basketball team. Such company teams were quite common during Jackson's booming post-war days.

Clark Equipment officers R.J. Burrows and Eugene B. Clark posed near the Clark Equipment Company's 'Autotram.'

The Clark Equipment Company's original Jackson plant — note the 'Autotram' parked behind the building. In 1950, Clark opened its new Jackson transmissions' assembly facility at 1300 Falahee road.

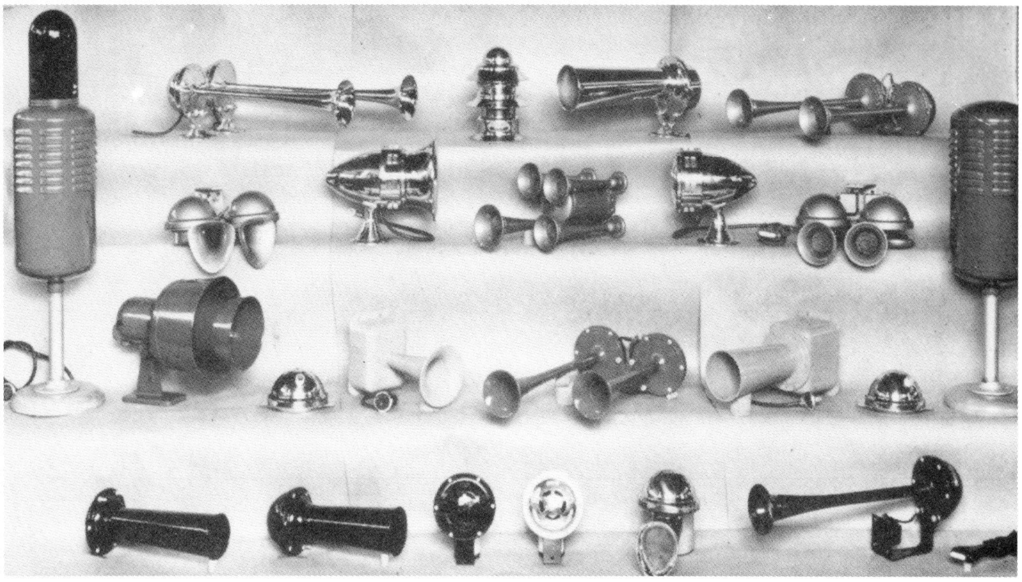

Sparks-Withington's 'Sparton' brand products changed considerably throughout the company's years of operation. This display of Sparton horns shows the variety of the company's 'automobile warning signal' products — the products that made Sparks-Withington famous. Sparton horns were standard equipment on many celebrated cars, such as the Ford Model 'A.' Later, particularly in the post-war years, Sparton began to diversify into other product lines.

Sparton

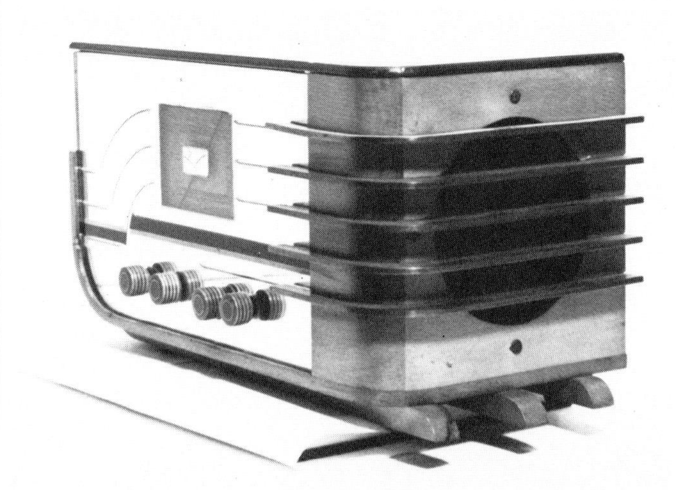

By the late 1930s, when the company began preparing for war contracts for both Britain and the U.S., the appearance of Sparton radios had changed dramatically. Though radio technology remained essentially the same until the 1950s, the design and appearances of radios changed dramatically. This 1936 Sparton radio, styled by industrial designer, W. Dorwin Teague, showed the influence of industrial streamlining that became even more popular after the close of the Second World War.

Sparks-Withington entered the radio manufacturing business quite early, making its first radio in 1925. This 1930 model contained both a radio receiver and a phonograph, but still looked like a finely-crafted piece of cabinetry or furniture.

In the fall of 1938, Sparks-Withington assigned a group of engineers the task of developing a television receiver and testing equipment for its production. The first Sparton television was finished in 1939, but the onset of the war stalled its mass production for almost six years.

Following the close of the war, television again became a Sparks-Withington product focus and T.V. grew more commonplace as a part of American life. Sparton continued to expand its line of television products in the early 1950s. This 1950 model Sparton T.V. shows the drastic change in the set's appearance that had occurred in less than ten years.

Although televisions had been expensive luxury items at first, the growing wealth of the post-war years and manufacturers' concentration on such luxury consumer items brought about a drop in the television's price. The use of mass-production techniques and assembly lines, such as the Sparton line shown here, made televisions a widely available product.

Goodyear

The Goodyear Tire and Rubber Company moved into Jackson just prior to the Second World War. Plans for the move were announced in 1937. Jackson's mayor and local industrialists welcomed the plant and its officials, hosting get-acquainted dinners in both Jackson and Akron, Ohio. Following the end of the war, Goodyear employed close to 1,500 people and was an important part of the city's economy until its move from the city in the 1970s due to economic pressures. Here a Goodyear employee is pictured operating the company's tire production machinery.

Yard-Man

Yard-Man, Inc. made lawn mowers and lawn care equipment. The company did a booming business in the years following the war, manufacturing mowers under the Sears Craftsman trademark until the late 1950s. Yard-Man employed hundreds of workers and profits and sales were high until the late 1960s. After changing hands twice in the early 1970s, the company ended production forever in 1975 when its assets were acquired by a Cleveland company.

Companies such as Camshaft, Dawlen, Jackson Drop Forge, Lefere Forge and Machine Company, Thorrez Industries, and Industrial Steel Treating were developed by men with the mechanical feel that comes from actual hands-on experience and working with machines and materials. These men, who had often worked for other larger companies, took an idea, hired a few skilled workers and opened a shop. Some companies such as Thorrez Industries and Lefere Forge weathered the lean years of the Depression and prospered during the Second World War. Others such as Camshaft, Dawlen and Industrial Steel Treating got their start during the war.

With the surge in technology that followed the war, new highly technical tools and machines were developed, allowing these companies to boost production and expand. These new machines had the instrumentation necessary to accurately measure and control precision procedures, as well as carry them out. The need for the problem-solving experience of the early craftsman began to fade.

This interior view of an unidentified, early Jackson machine shop gives an idea of working conditions and methods, ca. 1910. Workers at the mechanic's benches hand filed and formed parts to specifications and, often, the tools used were the mechanic's own.

In contrast to the earlier shop pictured above, this interior view of Industrial Steel Treating, ca. 1962, shows the changes in shop organization and the increased use of technical machinery. Industrial Steel Treating was opened by Charles St. John in the latter years of the war. In 1949 metallurgist, William Levy, joined the company and the small heat-treating company began to expand. A third generation of the Levy family is involved in the operation of this successful Jackson Company.

The William Bennett Business Block, later the home of the L.H. Field Company, as it appeared ca. 1895, at the corner of Jackson and Michigan Avenue. Many business blocks were built in Jackson's downtown area during the city's booming growth throughout the 1870s and 1880s. Prominent local capitalists and financiers backed their construction and many of the old blocks bore their names: the Calvert Block, the Goldsmith Block, the Kennedy Block and the Reynolds Block were joined by others like the Crystal Palace Block and the Marble Front Block. These commercial centers were to become homes to the many small retail, service and supply businesses that grew up around Jackson's industrial backbone.

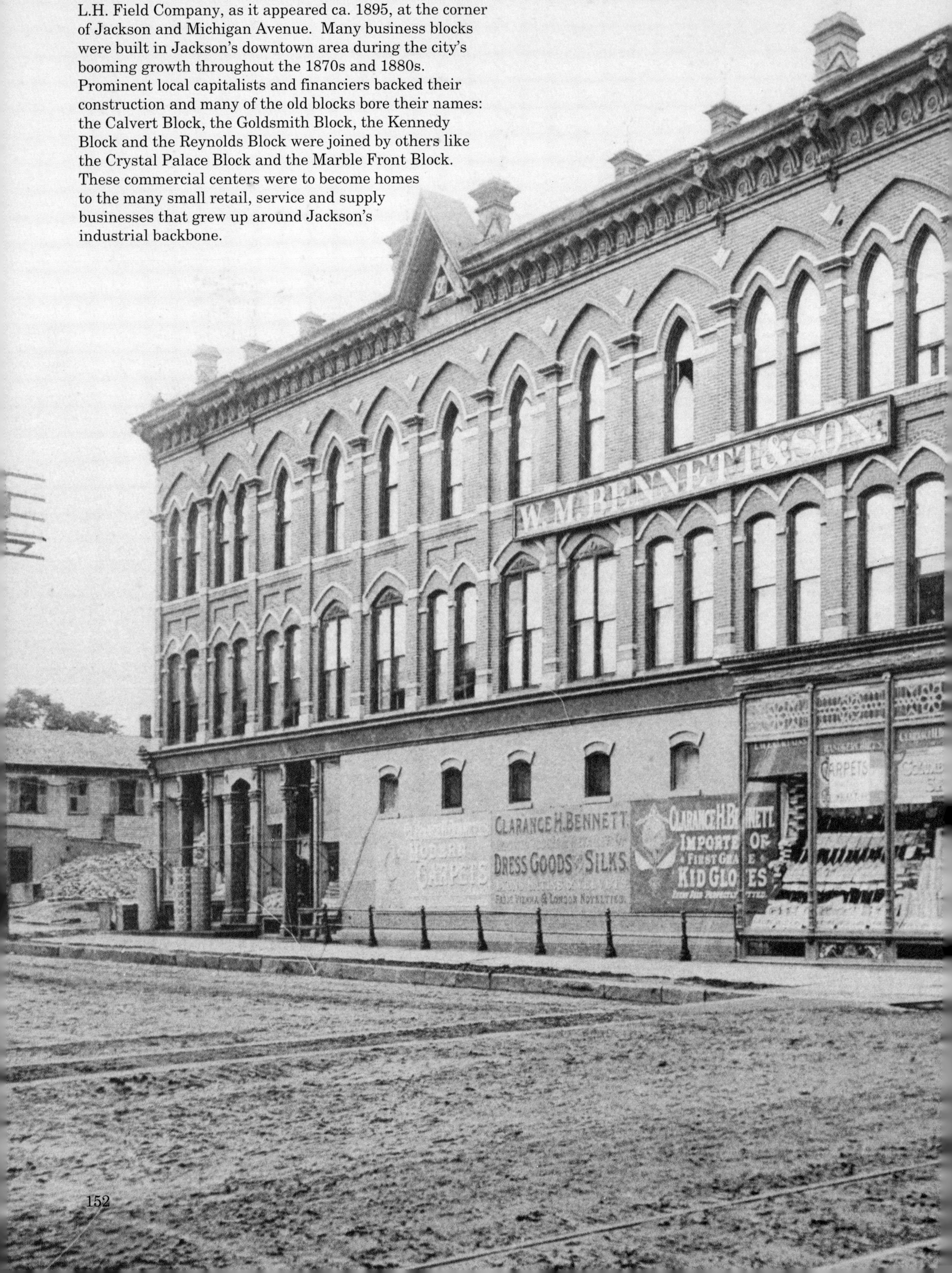

Jackson Retailing

The last section of this book is devoted to merchants and retailers of Jackson who, over the years, brought a world of products and services to their friends and neighbors. Many of these businesses are gone now and there has been much changed in the downtown skyline. Fortunately, change is good in the business world. It presents opportunities for new entrepreneurs and the creation of fascinating new products, ideas and services. Yet, it is fascinating for any Jackson citizen to remember the past and the way things were.

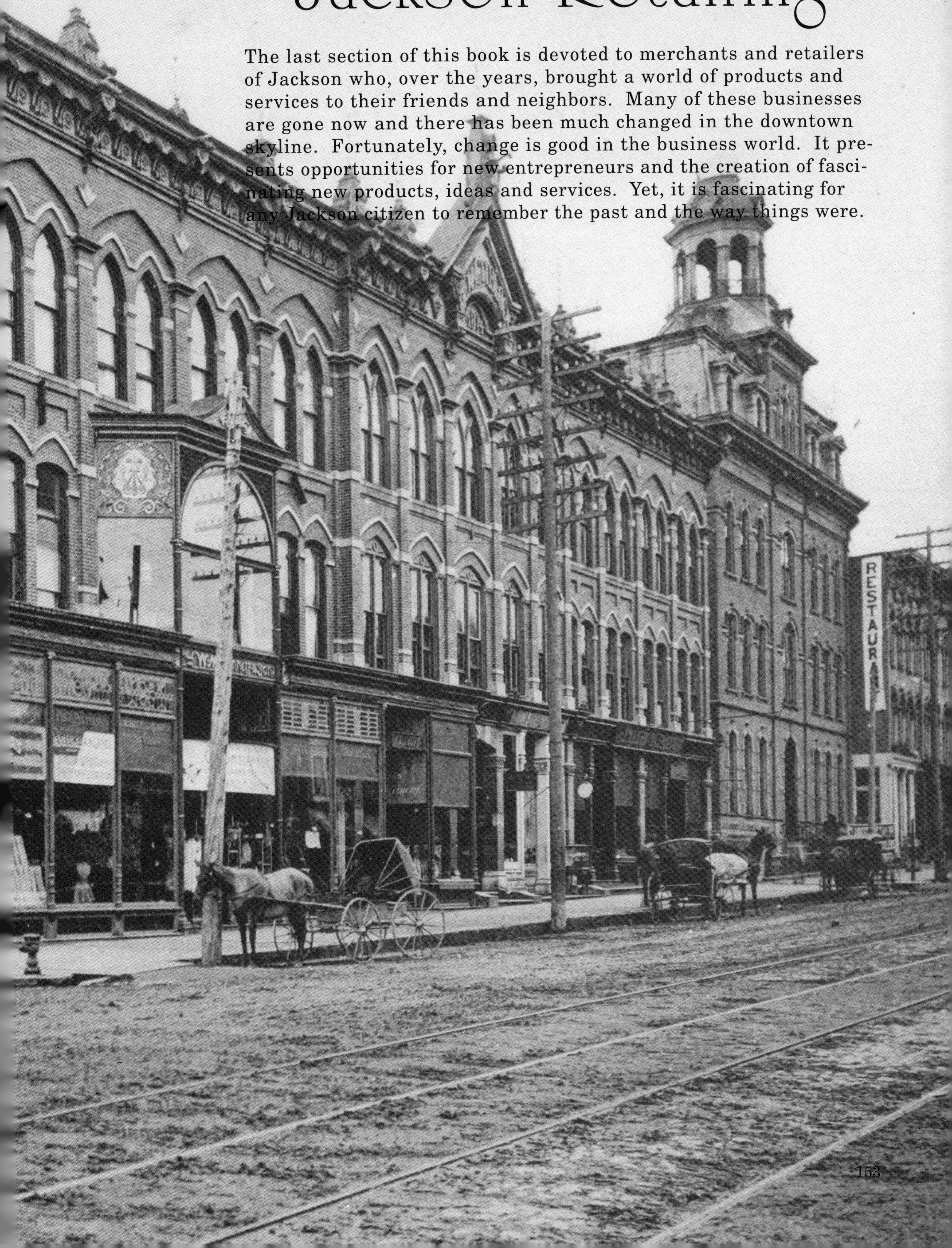

L.H. Field Company

Before the days of well-known national mail order and chain department stores, most cities were host to their own unique and traditional stores, merchant houses and dry goods services. Jackson's own L.H. Field Company had its beginnings in 1869 when Leonard H. Field opened a retail shop called the 'Busy Bee Hive.' Field's first store was located on Michigan Avenue, near where the City Hall stands today. The business grew quickly; the Busy Bee Hive was incorporated as the L.H. Field Company in 1891. By 1896, Field was looking to expand his store and he moved to a larger location in the William Bennett Business Block at the corner of Jackson and Michigan Avenue.

By 1904, business at Field's was booming and the company purchased the entire Bennett Block, which became known as, simply, 'Field's.' The store still maintained its small retail shop feel, however, for many years. In 1916, when an extensive remodeling project was begun, Field's expanded and re-designed the interior and exterior of the building, attaining the look of a modern, plushly finished department store: window displays, elevators, elegant lighting and new sales' services all became part of the Field's experience. It was around this time that William Field took over for his father, Leonard Field, as the head of the company. The younger Field remained in charge of the store until his death in 1925, and he was succeeded by Field's vice-president and partner, Fred F. Ingram. By 1929, other changes were in the air as well. Field's became affiliated with Hahn Department Stores, later reorganized as the Allied Stores. Jacksonians' experience of Field's didn't change, however: shopping at the store had become a local tradition and the store was noted for the uniform quality of its merchandise and for Leonard Field's policy of one uniform price for everyone.

Field's appearance remained essentially unchanged until the 1950s when a modernization and expansion program changed the store's facade and added a restaurant, customer accounts' offices, expanded window displays and an escalator. The escalator was Jackson's first and special introductory rides were given to the public. The store remained a part of Jackson life until the late 1980s when, after a consolidation with Herpolsheimers of Grand Rapids, the store was permanently closed.

Leonard H. Field, founder of the L.H. Field Company department store.

The L.H. Field Company's downtown Jackson store as it appeared in the night-time, ca. 1919.

An advertisement for Leonard H. Field's Busy Bee Hive.

A view of the interior of the L.H. Field Company store, ca. 1915.

Leonard H. Field posed with his family for this photograph, ca. 1900. Field's son, William Field (standing center), took over the Field's department store in 1915. William died in 1925, and he was succeeded by Fred F. Ingram. Two of L.H. Field's grandsons worked in the department store as well. Pictured here are Leonard Field III (back row center) and Van Duzee Field (front row center).

Jacobson's

A Jacobson's window display from their Jackson store, ca. 1940.

Nathan Rosenfeld

The first Jacobson's store was opened by Abram Jacobson in 1869, in Reed City, Michigan. It was a general store, carrying all types of merchandise, from crackers and flour to farm machinery and clothing. By 1904, Jacobson's son, Moses, started a second store in downtown Jackson. The new store concentrated exclusively on fashionable women's clothing and quickly became a popular shopping spot in the growing Central City. A new building at 113 West Michigan Avenue was completed in 1920 (above) and it wasn't long after that a second Jacobson's store was opened in Ann Arbor, quickly followed by a third in Battle Creek. Moses and William Jacobson ran the three stores as a partnership and Jacobson's Stores Incorporated grew to gain loyal, local followings.

Richard Jacobson, William Jacobson's son, had no interest in taking on Moses Jacobson's responsibilities following his uncle's death and William decided to sell the stores. In September of 1939, William Jacobson sold his business to Nathan Rosenfeld. Rosenfeld, with his brother, Zola, took over the Jacobson's stores and began an aggressive expansion project. New departments were added to the stores: children's wear, sportswear, shoes, millinery, luggage and eventually men's wear, furs, home gift items, restaurants and art galleries. The Rosenfelds opened new stores in cities throughout Michigan and they also adopted an innovative central distribution system. The new system stocked all of Jacobson's fashion merchandise in Jackson where it was priced, ticketed and distributed by truck to each individual store. The growing company's central management and warehousing operation in Jackson brought fashion buyers and advertising artists to Jackson and Jacobson's grew more and more to be an important part of the city's retailing community.

The Glasgow Brothers and Dack Dry Goods and Clothing Store was established in 1884 in Jackson's downtown, on Michigan Avenue near Francis Street. The three Glasgow brothers and their partner stocked fancy dry goods, clothing and shoes and for many years were a familiar sight in Jackson's downtown shopping district. Advertisements for the store listed carpets, curtains, furniture, chinaware, house furnishings, toys, shoes, ladies' ready-to-wear and books as stock items. Though stores that carried a wide range of goods in many departments are accepted as commonplace today, most earlier stores and shops carried a specialty line of specific goods.

The store of Central City Clothiers was located on East Main and was one of Jackson's largest clothing stores.

This location on Michigan Avenue housed several businesses. In 1892 it became the location of Cook and Feldher, a dry goods store. This building, photographed ca. 1930, was later Stillman's Dry Goods.

S.H. Knox and Company, a local dime store, was also a downtown Jackson store. A small sign in the lower left window reads "New Japanese China — 10 cents each."

Taylor's Bazaar, ca. 1885. This store was located at the corner of Michigan Avenue and Jackson Street.

A look at the interior of Maher Brothers music store on East Main, ca. 1900. Jackson's downtown shopping district was filled with small shops specializing in one or another type of stock and it was not uncommon for many customers to know shop owners on a personal basis.

FALL IS HERE

Don't wait until everyone else is ahead of you with a

New Fall Suit or
New Fall Overcoat

Hurry up and get into new togs when you will enjoy them the most.

SUITS, $10, $12.50 and $15
NIFTY HATS, $1.50 to $3

You'll buy better quality here at a lower price.
Investigate our money-saving bargains

FURMAN'S
265 East Main

J.D. Furman founded Furman's men's clothing store in 1912. The family-owned store has been a part of Jackson's downtown Michigan Avenue shopping district ever since.

This milliner's, or women's hat-maker's, shop was located at 177 West Michigan Avenue, ca. 1905. Hats, bonnets and head coverings of all kinds were the milliner's product and at one time were an essential part of any woman's outfit. Men, too, wore hats and the covering of one's head was considered to be an act of respect as well as a practical way to keep warm.

This photograph, ca. 1910, shows the work room of William H. Pittelco's tailor shop. Tailor-made clothing was much more common in the nineteenth century than it is today. Ready-to-wear, mass produced clothing became much more prevalent after the close of the American Civil War.

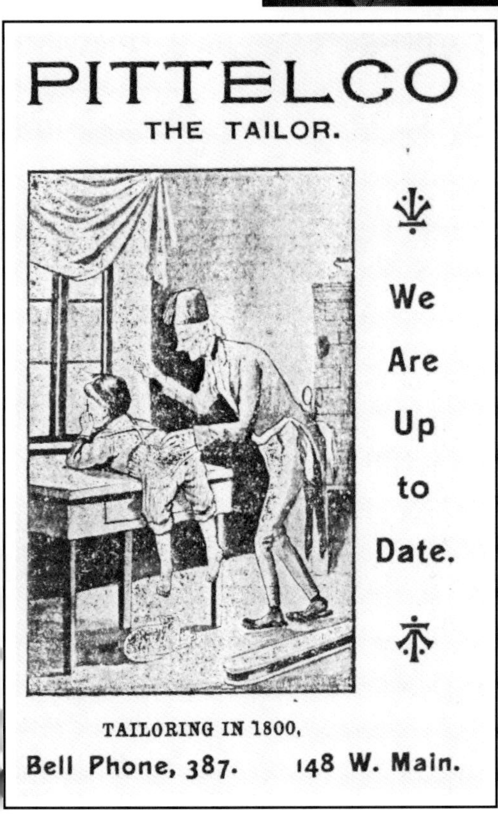

The Miller shoe shop was founded in 1915 and is still located in downtown Jackson on Michigan Avenue.

Shoes are one of life's least thought about but most noticed necessities. In 1917, Jackson was home to over twenty shoemakers who would custom fit and cobble shoes. Just as common, however, were retail outlets that carried pre-sized, mass produced shoes. One of the first such shops was the James Fallhee boot and shoe shop, shown here ca. 1885.

The photo below of the interior of the Walkover Shoe Store was taken in 1908. The man standing, far right, was the owner of the store, Mr. T.S. Rogers. The black patches hanging along the walls were leather samples, hung there to give customers an idea of what sort of leather was used in the various shoes offered by the store's inventory.

Small Retailers

The small shops of West Michigan Avenue, such as the three depicted here ca. 1885, eventually faded as larger stores carrying a more diverse stock located in and around the city. Larger stores could undercut the prices of small shops such as these, and with the increased competition, one or two businesses usually emerged as local leaders in specific lines of business. One example, the Smith-Winchester Hardware Store, became Jackson's largest. Established in 1864, Smith-Winchester continued to grow steadily and in 1905 the store was incorporated. By the 1950s, Smith-Winchester was distributing 900 page catalogs and had four different specialty warehouses in Jackson — a strong contrast with the small Michigan Avenue hardware showroom of J.C. Bader.

Pharmacies

Among the many service industries that made their homes in Jackson were the pharmacies. Businesses like The Chemist's Shop and the Flat Iron Pharmacy were important outlets for patent medicines, prescription medicines and other health aids. Before the days of the multi-function supermarket or the shopping mall, pharmacies located in local neighborhoods and the downtown shopping district.

This photograph, taken in 1895, depicts the White Block in Jackson's early downtown. Dr. C. J. White's drug store was located here — one of Jackson's first large pharmacies.

The Johnson Brothers Pharmacy, located at 420 First Street, was another of Jackson's neighborhood pharmacies. Many small pharmacies also featured soda fountains or ice cream counters. This view of the interior of the Johnson Brothers Pharmacy, ca. 1958, depicts a once-familiar sight.

This building, which stood at the corner of Greenwood and First, was originally a small, neighborhood grocery store that eventually became a pharmacy. The building was purchased around 1919 by Mr. Newhouse and in 1929 the wooden structure was rolled across the street on logs to an empty lot, making room for the construction of a brick building at the Greenwood and First site. The new structure housed the Flat Iron Pharmacy — so named for the building's odd, 'flat iron' shape.

Foote and Jenks began as a drugstore in 1884. C.E. Foote and C.C. Jenks eventually expanded their business to include the production of perfumes and flavor extracts. The small company employed several traveling salesmen, who marketed the firm's products throughout the United States. Pictured are employees of the Foote and Jenks Company at their workplaces. The firm's various extracts, scents and perfumes were bottled and packed by hand.

F & J Flavoring Extracts engraving.

The Bowers Coffee Ranch opened at 125 N. Mechanic Street in December of 1910. The small shop sold roasted and blended coffees. Herbert Bowers' store was a favorite among Jackson's early moviegoers: people would stop into the shop to buy roasted nuts before going to the theater to catch the latest films. Coffees, nuts, black pepper, cocoa, spices and teas were all a part of the Bowers' stock.

Dairies

One doesn't often think of milk or cheese as business, but dairy products and the processing of raw milk are an entire industry unto themselves. In the nineteenth century, milk was delivered daily from small farm dairies by horse and wagon: the milk was carried in tin-lined steel containers and was dipped out by the ladleful into whatever sort of holding container the customer had. Since the milk was raw, it was usually consumed that same day — thus the daily delivery. But following the invention of the Pasteurizing process by Frenchman Louis Pasteur in the late nineteenth century, milk kept for longer periods of time without spoiling. And in the 1880s, the glass milk bottle came into use in New York. By 1900, use of the glass milk bottle to contain pasteurized milk for home delivery was widespread throughout the United States.

In Jackson, many small farm dairies delivered milk to customers throughout the county. But this was to change after the turn of the century. The milk bottle greatly increased the efficiency of milk distribution and also led to the invention of fast, efficient bottle washers and bottle filling equipment. The capital necessary for such equipment led to a greater centralization into milk processing centers away from farms and into urban areas. Similar to the adoption of the assembly line by many national manufacturers, many dairies in the 1930s and 1940s began to use larger amounts of mechanized equipment in the pursuit of greater efficiency. In Jackson, such centralization was common and many smaller dairies and milk process-

The Servall Dairy building at South Street and Brooklyn Road in 1948. Servall was started by C.B. Hayes, Ed Hetherwick and __ Gregory. In 1946, the dairy was sold to Harry Abbott and Oliver Sweitzer and Servall eventually purchased the Loud and Jackson Dairy to form Jackson All Star Dairy, Inc.

This Jenkins Ayrshire Dairy delivery truck ran a rural route. The Jenkins dairy was one of Jackson's smaller farm dairies, not a central processor. The larger, processing plants didn't actually milk any cows: milk was purchased from smaller dairies and paid for by the pound, transported back to the processing center, packaged and then shipped out once more for retailing.

The Loud and Jackson Dairy milk processing plant at 1401 Daniel Road. Notice horse-drawn wagons on left and motor vehicles on right.

ing centers became consolidated into several large organizations. The largest of these, Jackson All Star Dairy, Inc. grew from many smaller dairies, including Servall Dairy, Loud and Jackson and Electropure Dairy.

Much like an industrial merger and acquisitions history, Loud and Jackson's past includes the continued absorption of many smaller farm dairies and milk processors who were forced out of the business due to bankruptcy, increased competition or a willingness to sell. Home delivery of milk fell off in the 1960s with the rising costs of insurance, pensions and other assorted business expenses. Jackson County's last large dairy, the Jackson All Star Dairy, was sold in 1991 to Roelof Dairies of Galesburg, Michigan: the largest continuously owned and operated dairy processor in the state of Michigan.

The bottling room of the Loud and Jackson Dairy, ca. 1950. Mechanized processing of milk and milk poducts pushed the centralization of many of Jackson's smaller dairy farms and processors into larger, factory-like milk production centers.

This 'Ellen and Jay' Loud and Jackson milk flag was used by customers well into the 1950s to indicate which products the milkman was supposed to deliver. The color codings allowed the milkman to be able to see which products were needed before he exited the truck.

This dairy case from the old Loud and Jackson Parlour was filled with the dairy's various products.

The Loud and Jackson Dairy Bar

Groceries

The Parker and Fleming 'wholesale grocery' was originally located in the old Bennett Block in downtown Jackson. Like many of Jackson's older style of grocery stores, Parker and Fleming sold many of their 'goods' unpackaged, relying on customers' own bags, wrappings or containers.

J.F. Sauer and Company was another small grocer in downtown Jackson. Their store, pictured above ca. 1890, was located at 204 East Michigan. The son of the store's founder, Dan Sauer, worked as a clerk in the store and later became a mayor of Jackson. Neighborhood grocery stores such as Sauer's often served as meeting and visiting places as well as grocery stores.

The J.L. Parkinson and Company store, pictured here ca. 1884, was at 115 South Jackson Street. In 1890, the small neighborhood grocer moved his stock and business to Chicago.

The Seamans Brothers grocery store was run by brothers Frank, Fred and Tom. The Francis Street store, pictured here ca. 1885, was a popular neighborhood grocery. Before the widespread introduction of the automobile, most people shopped for groceries and other household needs within walking distance of their homes. Neighborhood stores often grew to be tightly-knit meeting places for local residents. Smaller, local grocery stores grew to be less popular with the introduction of the supermarket. The centralization of many different types of products, from vegetables to household cleansers, under one roof meant cheaper prices due to higher volumes. People could reach the supermarket by automobile and the neighborhood grocery store slowly faded away.

This building, reputedly built around 1853, was at High and Belden streets and housed, among other things, a small grocery store.

The Snyder Brothers grocery store, ca. 1900. James and Lawrence Snyder's grocery was nestled into the corner of Lansing Avenue and Clinton Road. The store sold all sorts of things, and as the sign above the door indicates, they were noted for 'square dealing.' A new Snyder Brothers store was built across the street in 1927 and it stayed in the family until the late 1960s. Note the early gas station and price of gasoline at 28.9 cents per gallon.

Workers at the Homade Food Market pose before their Michigan Avenue store in 1932.

The market was sort of a step between the neighborhood grocery and the larger, less personal supermarket. Many local residents remember the Homade Market as a friendlier, more casual place to shop. The Homade sold an entire range of groceries, but also included a catering service as well as a small dining area.

Henry's Pure Food Shop sold fresh vegetables and fruits as well as health foods and packaged groceries. The small grocer was on West Michigan Avenue, across the street from the Hotel Hayes. This photograph of a fruit and vegetable display dates from the 1920s. The store later moved to Greenwood Avenue.

FLORIST

Brown's Floral Shop was founded in 1865 by Elbert and Clara Brown. The early floral shop, at 402 Greenwood Avenue, was called 'Idlewild Greenhouses.' Following the death of Mr. Brown, his wife, Clara, continued to run the shop and by the turn of the century, Fred Kempf and his family had joined her in running the business. Kempf eventually bought into the shop and took over its management. The Kempf family has run the store ever since, and continues to do so even today. This photograph portrays the Kempf family as they stand outside of the Greenwood Avenue greenhouse, ca. 1905.

Furnival's Flowers and Gifts was established in 1910 by Albert W. Furnival and his son. This 1910 photograph depicts the florist's first delivery wagon. In 1949 Gilbert J. Furnival joined as a third generation owner. The business continues today in the same location and is run by the fourth generation descendents of Albert Furnival.

Barbers

A nineteenth century Jackson barber, ca. 1885. Note the sign in the window advertising haircuts for fifteen cents. The windows on the second story have had towels tacked into the frames to act as screens — a common nineteenth-century practice.

Among the many service businesses that grew in demand as Jackson's population grew, was that of the barber. The England and Driscoll barber shop (shown here ca. 1885) was at 232 East Michigan Avenue.

In early twentieth century Jackson, service industries such as haircutting were often the province of African-Americans. The shop shown in this photograph, ca. 1910, was owned and operated by Jacksonian, Robert Green. Green's shop was north of Michigan Avenue on Jackson Street. Customers in the shop were whites only. Jackson laws dictated that either blacks or whites only could be served in any haircutting establishment. Green cut hair for white Jacksonians during the day and cut hair for black friends after hours.

Cleaning

H.S. Schafer founded his dyeing and cleaning service in 1900 at 217 South Mechanic. A special feature of the laundry was its exclusive automobile delivery service.

Cleaning services also became prominent in Jackson near the turn of the century. Establishments like the White Laundry, H.S. Schafer's Dyeing and Cleaning and the Wolverine Laundry Company grew to service Jackson's laundering demands. The Lee Tung family, Asian immigrants, ran laundering services, for a time, in turn-of-the-century Jackson. The White Laundry was established in the 1890s and employed almost fifty women and nearly twenty men in processing thousands of bundles of laundry every week.

The Star Carpet Cleaning Works performed laundering services of another kind. Using 'compressed air appliance and vacuum cleaners,' said a 1912 promotion, the Star Cleaning Works 'is in a position to execute thoroughly and promptly all orders for cleaning rugs, carpets, draperies, etc.'

Newspapers

The growing complexity of Jackson's commercial world and the inter-connecting business community naturally welcomed new communications technology to the community. Newspapers were informative traditions in Jackson almost from its very beginning, but telegraphs, telephones, radio and, eventually, television, all grew to be part of the day-to-day business needs of the city's shops, factories and services.

This picture of the Patriot Press Newsboys' Band was taken in the early 1900s on the steps of Jackson's old post office, the southwest corner of Mechanic Street and Washington Street. The *Patriot Press* had its beginnings as the *Jackson Patriot* in the late 1840s. The paper, notedly Democratic, was edited by Wilbur F. Storey in its first few years, and it grew to be a regular part of Jackson daily life. Storey later became the owner of the *Detroit Free Press* and he eventually gained control of the *Daily Chicago Times*.

The staff of James O'Donnell's *Daily Citizen* posed for this picture in the early 1900s. O'Donnell operated the *Citizen* from the mid 1860s until 1905, when he sold the paper to John George Jr. of Jackson and Ralph H. Booth of Detroit. The two men merged four of Jackson's papers, leaving the *Jackson Citizen Press* and the *Jackson Patriot* respectively. Nearly fifteen years later, John Miner sold the *Patriot* to Booth Publishing Co. and the paper we know today as the *Jackson Citizen Patriot* was launched.

Jackson telephone service operators, ca. 1885. These women plugged in and removed the connections between Jackson's earliest phone users — operators were contacted on every call and the connection between two telephones was made manually.

Jacksonians were some of the first Michigan residents to experience the seeming magic of the telephone. In 1879, services were started in the city for subscribers. Pictured here is a Michigan Bell telephone installation and repair crew, ca 1895. They stand before what was the city's red brick telephone building on Cortland.

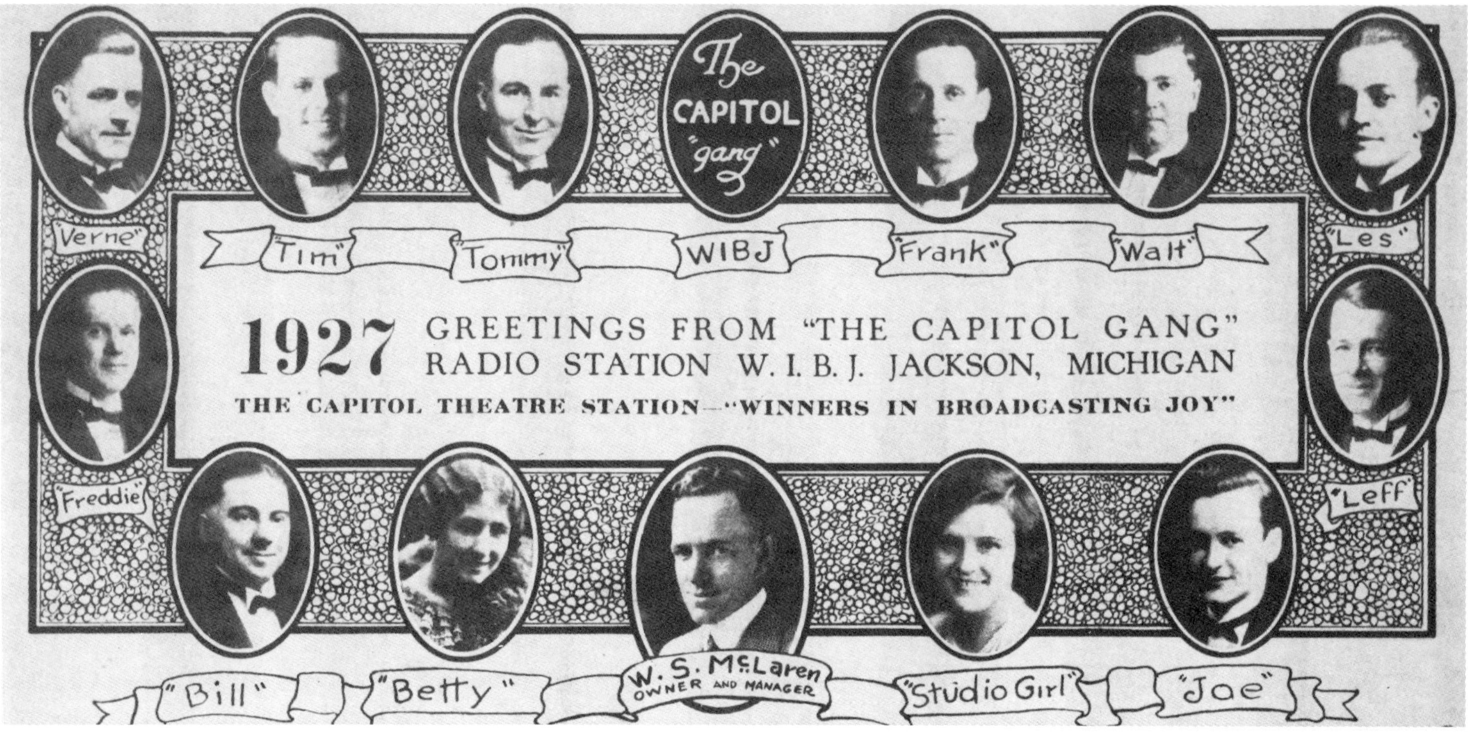

Jackson's first radio broadcasting business ran from studios located in the basement of the old Orpheum-Capitol theater. The 'Capitol Gang' became a regular part of the day for Jacksonians in the 1920s.

By the late 1930s, radio had become commonplace even in rural homes. The Jackson Radiomen's Association (pictured below in this 1937 photo) was a group of radio dealer, maintenance and repair shop owners. From left to right are Jim Foy of Foy Radio; Rennie Parkinson; Bob Hopkins of Hopkins Radio Shop; and Ken Parker.

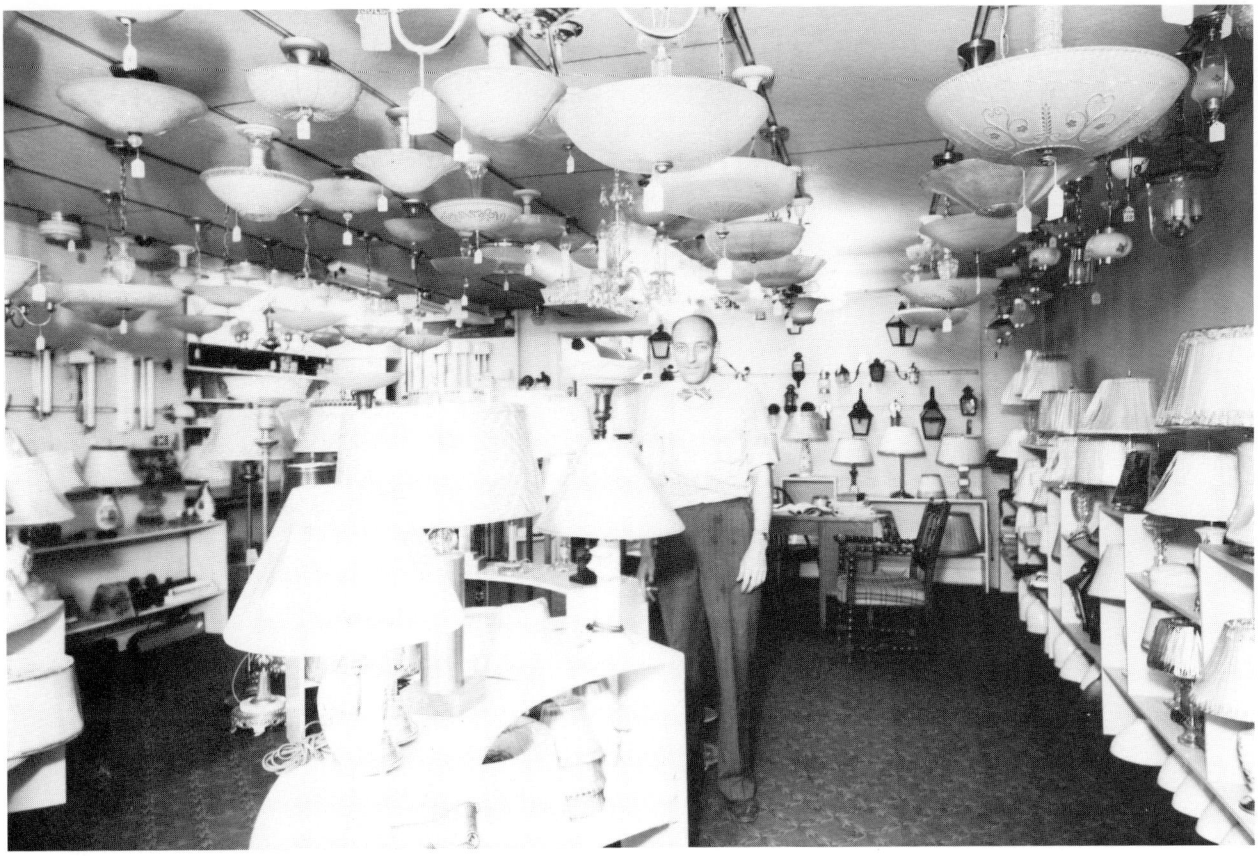

Beffel Lighting

Many Jackson businesses were family owned and operated from the very beginning. Two of the many that are still in operation are Beffel Lighting and the Toy House.

In 1927 Earnest Beffel opened the Beffel Lighting Fixture Company at 138 W. Cortland Street. Mr. Beffel had previously worked with his father's furniture store, Leonard Beffel & Sons. Ernest Beffel was a metal craftsman as well as a retailer and often did custom design and building of lamps and other architectural elements. The store (above) moved to its location on South Jackson in 1944.

A visit to the Toy House at Christmas and birthdays has been a tradition for many Jackson families since 1949. Philip Conley opened the store (below) at First and Franklin streets at an opportune time. The high birthrate in the years following the war combined with an increasing affluent population, created a huge demand for consumer goods such as toys. The Conleys moved the business to its present location on North Mechanic in 1967.

The Toy House

Street Scenes

This photograph of West Pearl Street was taken in 1895. Note the condition of the unpaved road.

# of Jackson

This view shows the south side of East Michigan Avenue, ca. 1895. From A.J. Brenk the 'Artistic Tailor' to C. Bartholomew's Dispensary, the many establishments that lined Jackson's main business district played a large part in the city's bustling downtown life.

Only a few years later, in 1908, Jackson's main street had changed very little. This view, looking East on Michigan Avenue, shows the trolley lines that made runs around the city's main thoroughfares. The Hotel Dalton is visible at the far eastern end of the street. Note the early streetlight at center top.

A view of Michigan Avenue, looking west, in 1905, during a parade.

By the 1930s, the appearance of Jackson's downtown area began to slowly change. Some of the old cobblestone streets remained, but Jackson's streets were increasingly home to the automobile. The horse and buggy, carriages and wagons had become a rarity. Taller buildings, making use of new construction materials, began to appear along Michigan Avenue. Here, a night view of the new National Union Bank Building, ca. 1930, shows some of the changes along what was once Jackson's busiest street.

Michigan Avenue 1940s

At the opening of the 1940s, many new businesses lined Jackson's downtown streets. The area remained a vital part of the city's commercial life and bustling groups of people, as well as lines of traffic, moved up and down

Michigan Avenue. These views of Michigan Avenue, taken in 1938, give some idea of the city's 'character' in those days. In several of these pictures, old business blocks from Jackson's booming 1880s are still standing.

Hotels

The Hibbard House, pictured here ca. 1895, was Jackson's first large hotel building. Many of the city's landmark events were celebrated in this facility, which was located at the southwest corner of Michigan Avenue and Francis Street, later the site of the Otsego Hotel.

Each of Jackson's hotels had a unique interior. This picture shows the Otsego Hotel's lobby magazine and cigar stand, ca. 1909.

The Hotel Hayes was built in the early 1930s and was supported by Jackson industrialists.

This interior view of the Hotel Hayes' ballroom shows the 1950 Sparton '500 Club' Dealers Meeting. Seated at the right side of the table, near the center, are Harry Sparks, Winthrop Withington, M.J. Corbett and Clifford Sparks. Many of Jackson's local industrial leaders, as well as private social clubs, used the Hotel Hayes as a meeting spot for gatherings such as these.

Banks

This portrait of Peter B. Loomis was taken in 1890. Loomis was one of Jackson's most influential early financiers. He moved into Jackson in 1843 and started a small dry goods business and later became the owner of the Kennedy Mills. In 1856, Loomis became a partner in a local banking firm which became known as P.B. Loomis & Co. Loomis helped in the administration of several Jackson railroads, was elected a member of the state legislature and served as one of early Jackson's mayors.

The Jackson State Savings Bank was located at 109 E. Main and was organized in 1896. This picture, ca. 1940, shows the bank's classical revival exterior and facade.

An interior view of the Jackson State Savings Bank, ca. 1900. Jackson's banks were a vital link in the city's commercial chain — by providing the capital needed to get machine-intensive industries off the ground, Jackson's banks helped push the city's growth.

Jackson's Union Bank was established in 1883, with William H. Withington as the bank's president. It was located at 177 West Michigan.

This building, above, at the corner of Michigan and Francis, originally housed the Central State Bank, but by 1942, it was known as the Security Building, housing Security Savings and Loan.

National Union Bank and Trust Building, at 120 West Michigan Avenue is shown in the photo at left.

City Bank & Trust Company, N.A.

City Bank & Trust Company, N.A. has the distinction of being the oldest continuously operating bank in the State of Michigan.

In 1848 George B. Cooper was granted a Michigan private banking charter, and founded what was to be the predecessor of City Bank and Trust. William D. Thompson joined in partnership in 1851 and the Bank was reorganized under the name of Cooper, Thompson and Co., Bankers, located on what was then West Main Street.

Just after the close of the Civil War, in 1865, a State Charter was issued to the Bank under the title Jackson City Bank and remained as a partnership until 1896 when another private Jackson bank owned by Peter B. Loomis was merged with the Bank.

The Bank once again changed its name to Jackson City Bank and Trust Company in 1927 to reflect the introduction of a complete trust department. Soon after, the Bank moved into new headquarters at 161 W. Michigan Avenue, diagonally across the street from City Bank's first home.

Beginning in 1952, the Bank began a rapid succession of growth in neighborhood branch offices and acquisitions. The first merger was with the

One of the first homes of what was to become City Bank and Trust Company, N.A. on W. Main Street in 1888.

Elegant main lobby of the City Bank and Trust building located on W. Michigan Avenue in 1927.

Commercial and Savings Bank of Albion in 1955. Since that time the Bank has continued to expand through mergers in both Homer and Springport, and in 1965 the name change to City Bank and Trust Company, National Association was finalized.

The current headquarters of City Bank and Trust was built in 1971, in an office complex at One Jackson Square, constructed on an urban renewal site in the heart of downtown Jackson.

In 1981 the Bank formed its own holding company, CB Financial Corporation and continued to acquire banking companies. The Clinton Bank and Trust Company of St. Johns was acquired in 1983, the Charlevoix County State Bank in 1992 and the most recent acquisition of the First State Bank of Charlevoix in 1993. The two Charlevoix banks merged in October, 1993, to form the subsidiary CB North.

CB Financial Corporation continues to seek opportunities for growth throughout the State of Michigan and provides full financial services to those communities in Northwest and Central Michigan.

This impressive structure at 161 W. Michigan Avenue served as the bank's home for 50 years.

Current headquaters of City Bank and Trust Company, N.A. and its holding company, CB Financial Corporation. The facility was built in 1971.

It Wasn't All

The people who owned and worked in the numerous companies in Jackson also contributed to its social climate. They were the city's boosters. They belonged to the numerous service organizations, took advantage of the area's recreational facilities and organized golf and boating clubs. They went to local theaters, supported musical groups, and organized parties, dances, and theatrical "Follies." In short, they had fun!

In the photograph below a group of Jackson business and industry leaders gathered for a costume party. Although we don't know the occasion, the names are familiar. How many do you recognize? Among the names on the back of

Work............

the photo are Jay Clark, Myrtle Jones, Stan Porter, Loraine Jones, Arthur Bloomfield, Irene Bisbee, Dr. John Smith, Rayner Field, Jim Wood, Hall and Louise Blanchard, Ethyl Smith, Roy Cornwell, Harry Sparks, Phil Kudner, Ken Weatherwax, Ruth Ingram, Zeph Potter, Otto Schultz, Russ Bengal, Cap and Tilly Sparks, Girt Seybold, Hugh Smith, Bud Ingram, Tucker North, Don McKone, Jerry Strong, Cliff Sparks, Bill Corbett, Berry Beaman, Bill Pittelco, Frank Ford, Harry Hancock, and many, many more …

From The Past To The Present

The appearance of Jackson's business and industrial districts changed drastically after the close of the Second World War. Unprecedented periods of growth in construction and industrial development helped to distribute a growing wealth and brought a surging demand for consumer goods and services. As America's wartime industries converted over to peacetime production, many once-expensive products dropped in price. This was particularly true of the automobile. Cars had already significantly changed most American cities by the 1930s, but the manufacturing needs of the Second World War temporarily interrupted their production. With the close of the war, cars became the most popular form of transportation, eclipsing interurban lines, city streetcars and even trains. The renewed popularity of the auto helped to change national and regional patterns in land development. These new patterns brought noticeable effects to Jackson.

One of the most significant of these was the widespread buying of smaller, often pre-fabricated homes in more rural areas. Cities like New York, Chicago, Detroit and Los Angeles experienced an intensive suburbanization and, like these larger urban areas, Jackson grew increasingly suburban as fewer and fewer people chose to live in the older, established living areas within the city. Many Jacksonians preferred, instead, to move to more rural wooded areas, made increasingly accessible by the widespread use of the automobile. The suburban homes that had once been a luxury enjoyed by only the very wealthy, became increasingly available to more and more people and the construction of new homes in outlying areas altered Jackson's long-standing appearance. This change in living patterns brought with it a similar change in the locations and types of business and industry within the city.

Shopping areas that catered to Jackson's subur-

This photograph represents the passage of time as well as any in this book. Some Jacksonians still remember cold icehouses, fearsome ice tongs and delicious slivers of refreshing ice chipped off a huge block of ice. It just sounds better than ice cubes in a plastic bag at the convenience store.

bians began to appear within the center of the more heavily populated outlying areas, undermining the importance of the downtown shopping district. Large supermarkets and multi-purpose grocery stores began to take the place of smaller neighborhood and local markets, and many national, chain retail stores began locating in Jackson. Gasoline and service stations began to dot the city's roadways. By the late 1940s and throughout the 1950s, many of Jackson's businesses moved toward the city's perimeter in an attempt to remain convenient and accessible to consumers and workers. Although many shops founded in the downtown area continued to thrive there, new businesses and commercial growth steadily moved further away form Jackson's downtown.

Similar changes occurred in Jackson's industrial districts. Large industry's increased use of diesel trucking after the war lessened the importance of location near a railroad or track-switching center and it opened up new vocational possibilities for industrial developers. Though many of the city's industrial sites continued to thrive, a noticeable trend saw new factories located further from the city. Most noticeable of these were factories locating in the new Micor Industrial Park, on Jackson's southeast side. Such developments increasingly took advantage of Jackson's connection to the I-94 Chicago-Detroit corridor for the distribution of goods, and the availability of land.

Change is inevitable. Over the years large and small companies have opened and closed. The cities population has expanded and decreased. But the two factors that first attracted people to the area in the 1830s and continue to attract business and industry today, remains — available transportation routes and inexpensive, undeveloped land.

This book covers the time period from the cities beginning in 1830 until the 1960s. The history of Jackson business and industry continues. The story is far from being complete.

Aerial view of Jackson, Michigan.

Acknowledgements

A project of this type is not completed without a great deal of support. So, a special thank you to City Bank and Trust Company for sponsoring this publication. Their marketing director, Susan Burns, was great to work with. Brad Baraks, of G. Bradley Publishing, patiently met with staff every other week to give us much needed guidance and encouragement. Peter Blake, president of the Jackson County Historical Society, and Mary Youngdahl, volunteer extraordinaire, helped with proofreading. And, of course, the project would not have been possible without the support of the Ella Sharp Museum — its members, board, and staff. Thank you for the time, work space, financial assistance, and moral support.

To those companies and individuals who took the time to respond to our letters, phone calls, newspaper articles and personal pleas, we are most grateful. To those who discover material about a business or company after the book is in print, please preserve it carefully or consider donating it to an institution who can care for it and use it, such as the Museum. And I urge those of you who are in charge of companies or businesses today, to take time to photograph and record your history. It will be of vital importance in the future.

We were not able to include information about every company or to use all photographs submitted. We made every effort to insure historical accuracy, but often had incomplete information. We apologize for any omissions or inaccuracies.

Contributors

Harry and Mary Abbot
Margaret Artz
Ron Bean
Jack Beattle
Beffele Lighting
Donald Bender
The Bentley Historical Library
University of Michigan
The Max Brall Family
Brown Floral Company
Camp International
Thomas H. Clark
Dawlen Corporation
Dawn Food Products
R.H.Dedrick
Elizabeth Dorr
Carl Eberle
Ella Sharp Museum
Emmons Service Inc.
Furmans
Patty Freundl
Furnival's Flowers and Gifts
F.A. Gansmiller
Wellington T. Gideon
Edward Handley
Robert A. Hoffman
Jackson County Historical Society
Jacobson's
Bob Johnson
Tom Johnson
Robert andJean Kaupp
Jean Laughlin
LaVern Lindsay
Leo Miller
Dorothy Mitchell
The National Automobile Historical
Collections, Detroit Public Library
Terry H. Neill
Dale and Charlotte Newhouse
Marie E. Perrine
Pioneer Foundry
Jessie Pulse
Cheryle Scheele
Lynn Seamans
Sally Shaw
The Alfred P. Sloan Museum
Elsie Bowers Smith
Rita Snyer
Tompkins HistoricalSociety
Sperry Sparks
Bob Walker
Willbee Concrete Products
Frances Williams
Jake Zaski
James Zuleski

Ella Sharp Museum Publication Staff

Left to right
Gregg Larsen
Tom Bohn
Lynnea Loftis.

Bibliography

Annual Reports of the Bureau of Labor and Industrial Statistics 1883 - 1908; Robert Smith Printing Company State Printers and Binders; Lansing, Michigan.

Annual Reports of the Department of Labor 1910 - 1917; Wynkoop Hallenbeck and Crawford Co. State Printers; Lansing, Michigan.

Balfour, Arthur J.; "Automobiles Produced in Jackson, Michigan;" © 1982, unpublished research paper; Jackson, Michigan.

"Barbour Papers;" Bentley Historical Library; University of Michigan, Ann Arbor, Michigan.

Barnes, O.M.; "Our Prison Industries: Some Observations on the Opposition to Them and on the Various Modes Proposed for the Employment of Convict Labor;" a paper read before the Boards of Control of the State Prison, January 16, 1895; Ella Sharp Museum Archives and Collections.

Bush, George; *Future Builders: The Story of Michigan's Consumers Power Company*; © 1973, McGraw-Hill Book Co.; New York, New York.

The Citizen Industrial Edition; © 1889, *The Jackson Citizen*; Jackson, Michigan.

DeLand, Col. Charles V.; *DeLand's History of Jackson County, Michigan*; © 1903, B.F. Bowen Publishers.

Deming, Brian; *Jackson: An Illustrated History*; © 1984, Windsor Publications; Woodland Hills, California.

Dunbar, Willis; *All Aboard! A History of Railroads in Michigan*; © 1969, William B Eerdmans Publishing Co.; Grand Rapids, Michigan.

1874 Atlas of Jackson County, Michigan; © 1874, Everts & Stewart; Chicago, Illinois.

Eighth Biennial Report of the Michigan State Board of Corrections and Charities; © 1886, Thorp & Godfrey Printers and Binders; Lansing, Michigan.

Ella Sharp Museum Archives and Collections.

Elliott, Frank; "When the Railroad Was King;" *Michigan History*; V.49, #4.

Fuller, George; *Economic and Social Beginnings of Michigan: A Study of The Settlement of the Lower Peninsula During the Territorial Road Period 1805 - 1837*; © 1916, Wynkoop, Hallenbeck and Crawford Co.; Lansing, Michigan.

Headlight Jackson, Michigan: Sights and Scenes Along the Michigan Central Line; V.2, #7; © 1895, The Chicago Photo-Engraving Company.

History of Jackson County, Michigan 1881; © 1881, Inter-State Publishing Company; Chicago, Illinois.

Hill, Arthur S.; "The Romance of a Railway;" *Michigan History*; V.?, #?.

Hyde, Charles; *The Lower Peninsula of Michigan: An Inventory of Historic Engineering and Industry Sites*; © 1976, Wayne State University Press; Detroit, Michigan.

Jackson, Harry; *The Michigan State Prison, Jackson*; © 1928, The State of Michigan.

Jackson, Harry; *Statistical Report*; © 1933, The State of Michigan.

Jackson, Michigan 1912; © 1912, Jackson Citizen Press; Jackson, Michigan.

Joint Documents of the Senate and House of Representatives vols 1847 - 1880; "Report of the Joint Committee on the State Prison;" Bagg & Harmon State Printers; Detroit, Michigan.

McLaughlin, Doris; *Michigan Labor: A Brief History From 1818 to the Present*; © 1970, Institute of Labor and Industrial Relations — University of Michigan and Wayne State University; Ann Arbor, Michigan.

Message of Governor Stevens T. Mason to Senate/House of Representatives of the State of Michigan; © 1836, Morse and Bagg Printers; Detroit, Michigan.

Michigan Pioneer and Historical Collections; selected volumes; Wynkoop, Hallenbeck and Crawford Company; Lansing, Michigan.

Michigan State Prison Keeper's Diaries for 1857 & 1859, (anonymous); The Ella Sharp Museum Archives and Collections.

National Automotive History Collection; Detroit Public Library, Detroit, Michigan.

Pilcher, Elijah; "A Letter to the Joint Committee of the Legislature on the State Prison at Jackson;" from *Joint Documents of the Senate 1847*; © 1847, Bagg & Harmon Printers; Detroit, Michigan.

Polk's City Guide and Directory 1871-1950; © R.L. Polk & Co.; Detroit, Michigan.

Purves, J.H.; *The Nightkeeper's Reports 1882*; © 1957, Printing Department of the State Prison of Southern Michigan; Jackson, Michigan.

Santer, Richard Arthur; "Historical Geography of Jackson, Michigan;" © 1970, Ph.D. Dissertation, Michigan State University.

"Standard Time;" *Jackson Citizen*; December 11, 1883.

Thomas, James M.; *Jackson City Directory and Business Advertiser for 1867 & 1868*; © 1867, Carlton and VanAntwerp Printers; Jackson, Michigan.

"The Village;" *Jackson Patriot*; V.4, #21; September 7, 1847; p. 2.

"Working the Mines;" *The Sunday Morning Patriot*; V.32, #138; January 26, 1902.

DENTIST
SMOKE HOUSE
BOOKS
WALLPAPER

City Bank and Trust Company, N.A.

– BOARD OF DIRECTORS –

Harold P. Andrews
Chairman and Chief Executive Officer – Camshaft Machine Company

Brian D. Bell
President and Chief Executive Officer – City Bank and Trust Company, N.A. and
Director, Chairman, President and Chief Executive Officer – CB Financial Corporation

Clark E. Bisbee
President – Lee Bisbee Travel Service, Inc.

Douglas L. Burdick
Private Investor

Robert D. Craft
President – The Craft Agency, Inc.

Dale R. Dopp
Vice President of Finance and Management – Albion College

James N. Franklin
Vice President and General Manager – The Worthington Steel Company

Sherwood M. Furman
President and Secretary/Treasurer – Furman's Incorporated

Alvin L. Glick
Chairman and Chief Executive Officer – Alro Steel Corporation

Gene Haskett
Vice President and General Manager – Penske Speedways

Robert L. Johnson
Chief of Police – City of Jackson

Stephen J. Lazaroff
President – Diversified Precision Products, Inc.

Bernard H. Levy
President – Industrial Steel Treating Company

Phillip G. Miller
President – Miller Tool and Die Company

James F. Walker
President – J. F. Walker Co., Inc.

We have never claimed to be. "There are others." But, after repeated disappointments and "swear words," it is with a sigh of satisfaction and relief that a man looks at his perfectly laundered shirt, with its proper lustre and color, when sent home from our superior laundry. You can't beat it.

WHITE LAUNDRY,

115–117 Cortland Street East.

"QUEEN QUALITY" Oxfords make new friends continually, because for real beauty and comfort there are none to equal them. If you are looking for the very height of shoe style, coupled with absolute comfort and extreme durability, you will find all in "QUEEN QUALITY."

The picture shows a favorite style for this season; Kibo Kid; patent tip; light flexible sole; natty opera toe; medium high military heel; popular high wing circular vamp; fast color eyelets. Sizes, 2½ to 8; widths, A to EE.

Price, $2.50.

L. B COWLEY, 121 East Main St.

Men

"Let us all be up and Doing"

It seems logical to presume that smart clothes will assist you materially in any strides you may make, regardless of the direction. A fellow fittingly-garbed cannot be held back. His clothes give him confidence and gain him prestage.

Cause and Effect. Fashion Clothes

W. H. ADDISON & CO. MANUFACTURERS OF AWNINGS

THE MODEL

Varsity Suits

Same style as cut. Note broad shoulder effect, the close-fitting waist and the slight flare of the skirt. This is the ultra fashionable thing this season. Every young man who wishes to be in fashion should see these suits. Prices,

Hart, Schaffner & Marx Tailor Made Clothes

$10.00, $12.00 and $15.00.

J. N. TOOLE & SONS,

BOOTS, SHOES AND RUBBERS,

105 Main Street East, Between People's National and State Savings Banks. Southeast corner of Main and Mechanic Streets.

You are cordially invited to try our Footwear. Satisfaction Guaranteed.

CENTRAL CITY SHOE STORE

See our Shoes, Get our Prices, and we will Get your Trade.

Established 26 Years

East End Pharmacy

G. W. Austin, Mgr. Harry Johnson, Clerk

You say, "J.H.S. always has a good line-up on its team." We have a good line-up on

Drugs, Perfumes, Cigars and Candy

Come and see us. 1324 E. Main

¶ You undoubtedly know us as the Young Men's Store, the store young men look to, come to and plug for. We want you with us. Let's play the clothes game together.

Harrington's

JACKSON, MICHIGAN

"WHERE THE GOOD CLOTHES COME FROM"

EYES EXAMINED Scientifically and Without Charge

Heglund

108 S. Mechanic

Ladies,

in making your purchases of CORSETS and PETTICOATS ask for the Reliance.

TINKER & CHRIMES

HATS AND FURNISHINGS

Readers of the Reflector should reflect before purchasing their ... that Tinker & Chrimes reflect the most stylish goods that are brought to the city.

Jackson Steam Dye Works

J. A. DONALDSON, Proprietor.

Ladies' Dresses, Shawls, Sacques and everything in Silk and Woolen Goods Cleaned or Dyed, and Finished in a First-class Manner.

GENTS' CLOTHING CLEANED, DYED AND REPAIRED AND PRESSED TO LOOK LIKE NEW.

All Work Warranted. Orders by Mail or Express will Receive Prompt Attention.

115 WEST PEARL ST., JACKSON, MICH.

FLOWERS AND DESIGNS.

Fresh Flowers Always on Hand.

...rs. Blessing,

...358. 250 E. MAIN ST.

A HAPPY HOME FOR YOU

And a comfortable one too, if you come here for your Furniture and Furnishings. Everything to furnish the Home, complete. Sold at lowest prices in every way. Easy Payments if you desire

BREITMAYER FURNITURE HOUSE, 255-7 E. Main St.

British Medical Institute

103 Main Street East, White Block. Jackson, Mich.

TREATS ALL

Chronic, Nervous and Special Diseases

Thorough Examination and Advice, $2.00. Consultation Free.

Not open Sundays. Office Hours from 9 a. m. till 8 p. m.

DR. W. H. HALE, Chief Consulting Physician.

DR. E. L. WILKINSON, Chief Consulting Surgeon.

E. J. Van M...

serves the Finest Soda W... in the City.

Try it.

...155 M...

PURCHASE THE ELITE GLOVE-FITTING ADJUSTABLE TOP PETTICOAT

No Gapping No Bunching at the Waist

Made by JACKSON SKIRT & NOVELTY CO.

...evlin's Jackson Business College and Shorthand Institute.

...l or address

H. C. DEVLIN, Mngr.

GAGE & URCH, WOOD AND COAL,

209 N. Mechanic Street. Telephone 421.

Peoples' Shoe Sale

Cowley's Shoe Store, 121 East Main St.

Dennis Machine Co.

MANUFACTURERS OF HIGH GRADE BICYCLES,

314-316-318 N. Jackson St., Jackson, Mich

Smith Bros. & Collins Transfer Co.

Our Central Location in Jackson enables us to make the Quickest Time with the Least Freight to More Stations than any other Transfer House in Michigan.

There are Nine Railroads Running out of Jackson.

Michigan Central Going East.
Michigan Central Going West.
Michigan Central Air Line Division.
Jackson & Grand Rapids.
Jackson, Lansing & Saginaw.
Lake Shore & Michigan Southern.
Jackson & Fort Wayne.
Grand Trunk Railroad.
Cincinnati Northern.
54 Express Trains.
62 Passenger Trains, Arrive and Depart each day.

86 per cent. of all the Grain raised in Michigan is raised in the Four Southern Tier Counties.

Jackson, Mich.

"Jackson, the Hub of Michigan."

NEVER MISS DELUXE SPARK PLUG

Equip your Automobile or Motor Boat with one—they are guaranteed for one year

For Sale by all Garages

$1.00

Manufactured by Lockwood-Ash Motor Company

Cor. Horton and Main, Jackson

Compliments of Majestic and Rex Theatres

A. E. SUTTON, LIVERY, BOARDING, Exchange and Feed

...Waist Hats

...have just recived ...line of White ...Hats in new and ...able shapes. ...ry cool and comfortable for midsummer wear.

...& Sullivan

JOHN MALNIGHT, Importing Merchant Tailor

A Fine Stock of all kinds of Goods to select from. Satisfaction Guaranteed. As Good as the Best, and Cheap as the Cheapest.

Union Blk., cor. Main and Francis Sts., JACKSON, MICH.

USE JAXON SOAP.

Ask any of the merchants in Jackson for the RELIANCE PETTICOATS

They all have them.

Of course they must, for none can suit a well dressed lady better.

Ask to see them.

Respectfully,

RELIANCE CORSET CO.

BENNETT'S ART STORE and UNDERTAKING,

172 W. Main St. Phone 173

JACKSON HAT CO.,

Manufacturers of High Grade Stiff Hats,

111 E. Cortland St.

PHONE 975.

Gas is the Genius of Gastronomy

Some fires control you and your cooking; but you control a Gas fire to suit your cooking.

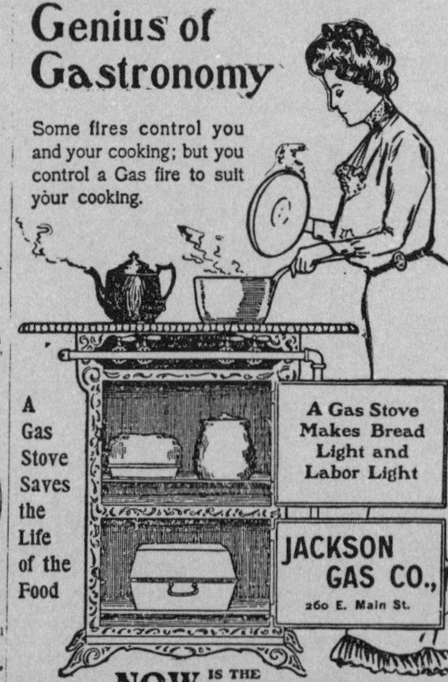

A Gas Stove Saves the Life of the Food

A Gas Stove Makes Bread Light and Labor Light

JACKSON GAS CO., 260 E. Main St.

BE SURE NOW IS THE TIME to Get a GAS RANGE

JAXON

The Best Soap ...

AFTER GRADUATION WHAT?

If you would be successful, look successful, wear clothes tailored to your individuality.

The clothes that we sell command attention, win positions and insure respect of your fellow men.

Appearance is as important as knowledge; with both you'll succeed

Smalley & Birmley

1412 East Main Street

Perfec... in Fi...

Correct fashion a... tory wear are w... in our Clothing, ... are lower than ... and quality any...

Rogers, ...

107 East Main.

ROBERT LAKE, CONTRACTOR AND BUILDER.

WHOLESALE AGENT

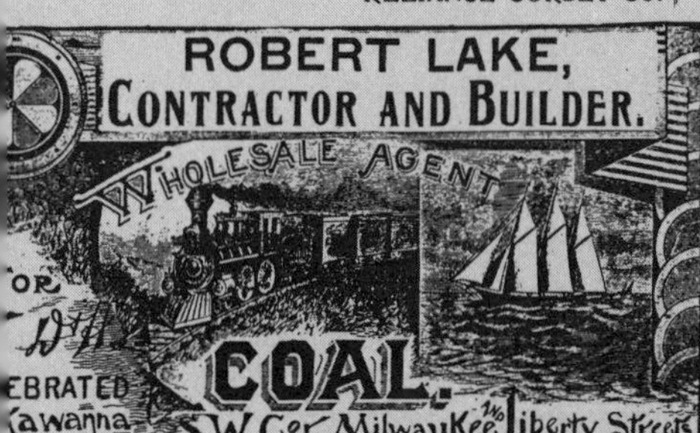

...EBRATED ...CAWANNA COAL.

S. W. Cor. Milwaukee and Liberty Streets

BUILDER OF PORTLAND CEMENT SIDEWALKS and CELLAR FLOORS.

S. W. Cor. MILWAUKEE and LIBERTY STREETS, - Jackson, Mich.

ALSO WHOLESALE AND RETAIL DEALER IN

Hard and Soft Coal, Coke, Lime, Portland, Louisville and Akron Cements, Plastering Hair, Common Salt, Roofing Felt, Tar, Pitch and Asphalt, Fire Brick, Fire Clay, Common Brick, Mortar Colors, Mineral Wool. Asbestos for Pipe and Boiler Covering, SMITHING COAL A SPECIALTY.

++ BRICK AND PLASTERING MORTAR. ++

BUSINESS OF BUILDERS AND CONTRACTORS SOLICITED.

MAIL ORDERS PROMPTLY ATTENDED TO.

EMPIRE DRILL CO.

Grain Drills, Fertilizer Drills, Plain Disc Drills, Fertilizer Disc Drills, Plain Spring Hoe Drills, Fertilizer Spring Hoe Drills, Plain Shoe Drills, Fertilizer Shoe Drills, Broadcast Plaster Sowers, Broadcast Fertilizer Drills, Broadcast Grain Attachments, Spring Tooth Harrow Attachments, Corn Planting Attachments, Sugar Beet Planting Attachments, Bean Planting Attachments, One-Horse Corn Planters with Blade Shoe or Wheel Coverers, One-Horse Fertilizer Drills, Garden Fertilizer Distributors, Horse Rakes.

Empire Drills are made in any size or style from an 8 to 24 Spring Hoe, Shoe or Disc, with or without fertilizer attachment. All drills are made with steel frame. Nothing better than an Empire Shoe, Spring Hoe or Disc Drill. We manufacture:

For prices, terms and large illustrated catalogue, which will be mailed free, address

EMPIRE DRILL CO., Jackson, Mich. C. McNOLTY, Mngr.

Jacobson's Garme...

Different than Ordinary

It is needless for us... allude to the high chara... of the garments carrie... our store, as almost ev... women in Jackson kn... the high standard of ... cellence they must at... to enter our department...

JACOBSO...

105 EAST MAIN ST...

FRANK PICKELL, Piano, Furniture and Safe Mover.

Headquarters, Grinnell Bros., Main St. Res. 127 N. Jackson St.

FURNITURE MOVING AND STORAGE TEL. 470.

CHARLES A. HOWIND, CONTRACTOR and BUILDER.

Manufacturer of Cement Walks, Cellar Bottoms and Tile Floors.

Estimates Furnished.

No. 15 Dwight Building, JACKSON, MICH.

M. C. BROWN,

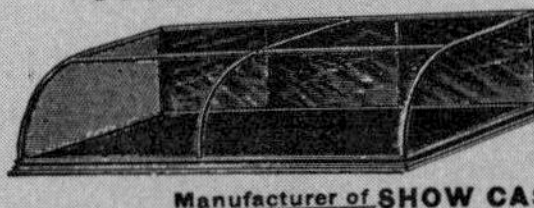

General Contractor and Builder

Manufacturer of SHOW CASES.

Office, Store and Bank Fixtures Built to Order.

Rear 167-169 W. Main St.

What Fashion Demands

in JEWELRY can be found here.

Whatever is designed and manufactured in the line of JEWELRY is made a part of our stock immediately.

We are especially well supplied with Watches and Diamonds; also Cut Glass, Art China and Silverware.

J. C. Moyers

Phone 532. 134 West Main

Get your --Summer Hat-- at O'Dwyer's.

They have the largest and most desirable stock at their usual popular prices.

171 Main Street West.

EAT RAMSAY'S CANDY. DRINK RAMSAY'S SODA.